Mali Political Instability,
West African Sahara State

Author
Daniel Roberts

Published
By
SONITTEC PUBLICATION.
2162 Davenport House, 261 Bolton Road.
Bury. Lancashire. BL8 2NZ. United Kingdom

Copyright Policy

Sonittec This Title is protected by Copyright Policy, any intention to reproduce, distribute and sales of this Title without the permission from the Title owner is strictly prohibited. Please when purchasing this Title, make sure that you obtain the necessary reference related to the purchase such as purchasing receipt. In accordance with this term, you are permitted to have access to this Title. Thanks for understanding and cooperation.

All-right reserved Sonittec ltd
Copyright 2020

Table of Content

TABLE OF CONTENT **5**

MALI POLITICAL INSTABILITY **1**

WEST AFRICAN SAHARA STATE **1**
Moving beyond the 2012 crisis 1
SUMMARY **4**
INTRODUCTION **13**
CHAPTER ONE **29**
A DIVISION TO NATIONAL UNITY, AS IT FAILED 29
CHAPTER TWO **65**
DESTRUCTION IN NORTHERN MALI, REBELLION OUTBRAKE 65
CHAPTER THREE **107**
FOREIGN POWERS INVOLVEMENT 107
CONCLUSIONS **133**
FINDING SOLUTION TO THE RECURRENT CRISIS? 133

Mali Political Instability
West African Sahara State

Moving beyond the 2012 crisis
About the roots of Mali's conflict report

This report constitutes the first research pillar of the new Maghreb-Sahel Programme of the Clingendael Institute's Conflict Research Unit, sponsored by the Dutch Nationale Postcode Loterij. It analyses the deep roots of the 2012 Malian conflict and explores the consequences of this crisis on Sahel stability and international involvement in the region. Despite several initiatives (Algerian mediation, joint efforts by the international community), the situation on the ground remains highly tense and is now threatening the stability of the entire region.

This in-depth study explores the long-term drivers of the Malian conflict and aims to highlight emerging trends that could question the effectiveness of international efforts in the Sahel.

Acknowledgements

The authors would like to thank all their colleagues from the Clingendael Institute's Conflict Research Unit, especially Rosan Smits, Ivan Briscoe, Jort Hemmer and Mariska van Beijnum for their invaluable assistance during and after the editing of this paper. We also want to acknowledge Janny Krayema for her outstanding availability regarding our numerous queries on articles and books. Very special thanks go to Virginie Baudais for her thoughtful peer review and the very high quality of her expert inputs. Finally, thanks for editing go to Paula McDiarmid and for typesetting to Textcetera. The contents of the report remain the authors' responsibility.

Summary

From January to April 2012, Mali underwent the fourth Tuareg uprising of its post-colonial history, an Islamist takeover of all the northern cities and an improvised military coup. This succession of destabilising events came as a surprise to all international observers, who long considered this country as a 'poster child for democracy in Africa'. In their view, deposed President Amadou Toumani Touré (ATT) appeared to shoulder the prime responsibility for the 2012 crisis. And while it is without doubt accurate to say that the former leader of Mali contributed in large part to the political degradation and worsening security conditions of the country, the root causes of the conflict are to be found elsewhere, predating ATT's presidency.

This paper, the first report of the new Maghreb-Sahel Programme of the Clingendael Institute's Conflict Research Unit, aims to explore the most prominent root causes and global influences that account for the 2012 crisis. It addresses the local issues that have played a significant role in undermining peace and security and explores the international dynamics that have contributed to this malaise. On the basis of that analysis, the paper seeks to give the many local and international bodies now engaged in the Sahel region, and in Mali in particular, food for thought as to what political, social and developmental challenges remain to be addressed so as to prevent a recurrence of armed conflict and institutional collapse. The paper should serve as a clear warning to all those who believe the international community can move on once the immediacy of crisis management in Mali has ended.

When Mali gained independence from France in 1960, the new government had to assert its authority on a large territory, including desert regions where Tuareg and Arab communities directly challenged its authority. This already difficult task proved to be even more challenging because of the deep resentment of Malian state officials towards sections of the northern populations whom they regarded as the main obstacle to national unity. The southern elites resolved to focus their political and economic efforts on the 'useful' south of Mali, gradually marginalising the north of the country and imposing military rule on those regions.

Simmering and historically rooted distrust had led to four Tuareg and Arab uprisings following independence: in 1963, 1991, 2006 and 2012. Even though peace agreements were signed and multiple demobilisation programmes implemented, none of them succeeded in normalising the relationship between the north and Bamako. Those repeated failures are, in part, a direct consequence of the Malian state's strategy of taming the north. In order to prevent one group from gaining too much influence and posing a threat to central state authority, Bamako sought to divide the northern 'front' and exploit interethnic and sectarian tensions to impose its authority. Among the instruments of this strategy were the use of electoral zoning to favour certain Tuareg tribes over other groups or the Arab community. Bamako also regularly employed ethnic-based vigilantes (Songhay and Fulani Ganda Koy or Ganda Iso, and today the Groupe d'auto-défense Touareg Imghad et allies (GATIA) movement) to counter the Tuareg and Arab threat.

The direct and long-term consequences of this counter-insurgency strategy were deep animosity between northern populations, fierce resentment by communities towards the central state, and a very heterogeneous distribution of needs and demands that made inclusive peace talks and agreements far harder to reach. Indeed, Tuareg, Arab, Songhay or Fulani northern people all have different political agendas, and do not share the same culture, political history, languages or traditions. They do not all recognise 'Azawad' as their common land, or the necessity of independence. Arabs and Tuaregs for instance, while not always opposed to Bamako, have long been in confrontation with the central state; the Fulani and the Songhay, on the other hand, have been far closer to Bamako, and have worked alongside the Malian regime for decades. The divisions between northern populations is a crucial element in understanding the difficulty in converting post-conflict stability into anything like sustainable peace.

Furthermore, intra-Malian tensions and community distrust have been aggravated by foreign interference and other, more passive, forces who have served to aid and abet tensions in the north. By taking advantage of the general weakness of the Malian state, these external actors have sought to build their influence primarily in the north.

The north of Mali indeed became a prize in the eyes of countries like Libya and Algeria, two regional powers that have long sought to push their agenda for Sahelian influence as a step to broader geopolitical primacy. Colonel Qaddafi attempted to garner the support of Malian Tuareg communities in order to fulfil his ambition of forming a League of Grand Sahara Tribes and impose himself as a continental leader. Alternating between promises of support for Tuareg rebellious endeavours and mediation in the aftermath of uprisings, he managed to establish Libya as a key player in Mali. Algeria, seeing the north of Mali as its natural backyard and a privileged territory in which to channel its own national insecurity (namely, Islamist terror groups), used its role as a regional counter-terrorist leader to assert influence in the northern regions. Over time, it challenged Libya as mediator in the aftermath of Tuareg uprisings.

Ethnic manipulation and foreign meddling were not the only signs of a state whose presence in Mali's north was partial, partisan and unpopular with many groups. Foreign charitable organisations, among them Arab-speaking non-governmental organisations (NGOs) and Islamic preaching movements, proliferated. Playing the role of social and security providers in the absence of a functioning state, Middle Eastern NGOs spread their own version of Islam within the north. This diffusion of new ideologies – mostly challenging the tradition of religious tolerance and Islamic syncretism cherished by southern populations – added another layer of tension and misunderstanding between the north and south of Mali. Southern populations have indeed held the northern tribes, especially the Arab and Tuareg, responsible for the growing influence of radical Islamic doctrines.

In the wake of the first hostage-taking activities in the Sahel, and the subsequent increase in attention on the country by Mali's Western partners, several international security and development programmes have been implemented. However, their exclusive focus on fighting terrorist and security threats in the Sahel, with limited consideration for other civilian issues such as economic development or social grievances, turned these programmes into accelerators of discontent and emblems of the negligence of public needs in the north. Moreover, weak ownership of these programmes by Malian counterparts, local embezzlement and a lack of regional cooperation have weakened the overall results of these efforts.

Introduction

The 2012 Malian crisis has placed Amadou Toumani Touré's regime in the dock of history. Accused by many, both inside and outside the country, of being the chief culprit for the breakdown of his country, President Touré has at times appeared to be the sole scapegoat for the conflict.

However, the crisis of 2012, which will be recounted briefly below, was also undeniably the result and most recent manifestation of Mali's political history as well as the long-standing distrust between different ethnic communities. Economic frustration, political resentment and strategic opportunity-taking, all of them rooted in the fragmented nature of the country, played a significant role in the crisis. As a result, any effort to achieve sustainable peace now needs to address not just the immediate run-up to the latest armed conflict in the country, but also the conditions that account for the recurrence of crisis.

The 2012 crisis: the fissures of a united insurrection

On 17 January 2012, three years after the last north-south peace agreement in Mali, a fourth 'Tuareg' rebellion was launched through the attack on a Malian military garrison in the north-eastern town of Menaka. Contrary to previous attacks, the rebel combatants seemed better prepared and organised, and above all appeared to have much more equipment than their predecessors, boasting 'the most impressive arsenal ever seen in the north of Mali'.

The National Movement for the Liberation of Azawad (MNLA), created in October 2011 by former Tuareg exiles in Libya, succeeded in gathering all the rebellious factions that had been divided and weakened by political disputes over time. As a result, the MNLA managed to represent all the main communities of the northern regions of Mali. The accidental death of the MNLA's chief instigator, Ibrahim ag Bahanga, in a car accident in August 2011 near Kidal could have endangered its military plans and encouraged new divisions. However, neither his death, nor Iyad ag Ghali's failure to impose himself as the political leader of the MNLA, undermined the planning that led to the January 2012 rebellion. Iyad ag Ghali, an historic figure of the Tuareg movement, was one of the key negotiator in the conclusion of the 1992 National pact. His stance in the negotiations, mainly advancing the interests of his own clan, coupled with his rampant radicalisation during the 1990s, had lost him the trust of other Tuareg communities.

By the end of April, the northern cities of Aguelhoc, Lere, Tinzaouatene, Tessalit, Kidal, Timbuktu and Gao were controlled by the rebellion. However, the MNLA was not able to preserve Tuareg and Arab unity. A few days after the first military operations, a new Tuareg group called Ansar Dine was created, led by Iyad ag Ghali. Contrary to the MNLA's military and political commanders, Iyad ag Ghali had a long and varied role in Mali's history of rebellions, of particular note is his alleged collusion with the Al Qaeda in the Islamic Maghreb (AQIM) movement.

Soon after the emergence of Ansar Dine in northern Mali, the nature of the rebellion changed and the MNLA began to lose its influence. While Tuareg rebel groups were first supported by Ansar Dine in their military takeover of northern cities, the MNLA progressively became the enemy of Iyad ag Ghali's new coalition. On top of fulfilling his own leadership ambitions, ag Ghali and his Ansar Dine movement sought to implement sharia law and to rehabilitate the authority and leadership of the religious elders, the Ulema. Helped by AQIM and the Movement for Oneness and the Jihad in West Africa (MUJAO), Iyad ag Ghali rapidly took over control of the rebellion. At the same time, he abandoned the political objective of independence for the Azawad region proclaimed by the MNLA. The occupation of all the major towns in the north led to the establishment of a new order based on, for instance, the creation of an Islamic police force in charge of enforcing new religious rules (on clothing, or the banning of 'secular' practices like smoking or playing football) or removing all un-Islamic 'vestiges' (bars and clubs, as well as the polytheist mausoleums in the town of Timbuktu).

A coup in the south

While the northern regions were going through an unprecedented security crisis marked by the split of the most important rebel movement, the general situation in Mali suddenly deteriorated following an improvised military coup on 22 March 2012. From the beginning of the Tuareg rebellions and the first casualties suffered by the Malian military, public discontent grew, especially in Bamako. Mothers and wives of southern soldiers fighting on the northern front protested against the poor condition of the military. Poorly equipped, badly trained and irregularly paid, Malian soldiers – mostly southerners – had always feared fighting in the north, some 1,400km away from their homes or families. According to one analyst, 'For a southern soldier from Sikasso or Kati, being sent up north to patrol the open desert is akin to a Muscovite being sent to Siberia in the 19th century.'

Popular historical anger against the 'armed bandits', traffickers and smugglers of the north was compounded by resentment against the Malian authorities themselves. Denounced by the military as the main culprits behind the impossibility of quelling the rebellion, the Ministry of Defence, the military chief of staff and ATT were at the centre of popular discontent. On 21 March, low and middle-ranked officers from the Soundjata Keita military camp in Kati (16km from Bamako) mutinied. They decided to go straight to the Koulouba presidential palace, where red berets from the presidential guard briefly resisted before finally abandoning their position after President Toure's evacuation around 9pm. On 22 March, Green Beret Captain Sanogo, aged 40, appeared on the national television channel ORTM as the head of a new military 'Comité national pour le redressement de la démocratie et la restauration de l'État' (CNRDRE). Kati putschists suspended all Mali's democratic institutions, and even arrested some of the main political leaders, with the exception of Ibrahim Boubacar Keita.

At the end of March 2012, Mali thus faced two critical political and security threats. On the one hand, half the territory was controlled by Islamist groups, governing through different rules and law and offering no recognition of Bamako's constitutional authority; on the other hand, a military junta had seized power in the south, imprisoned most of the legitimate authorities, and called for revenge in the north. Confusion was at its peak and only international diplomatic pressures enabled the restoration of apparent political order on 6 April. On the same day, however, the MNLA unilaterally declared independence of the Azawad region.

Mali's multiple crises brought into serious question the political regime's strength and the real popular adherence to national unity. For years, the country had been commended for its democratic transition, institutions and overall political progress. Labelled by many international partners as the 'poster child for democracy', Mali was depicted as an example for the entire African continent. What the 2012 crisis appeared to reveal, however, was a giant fraud by the Malian political regime, especially since the election of Amadou Toumani Touré in 2002 and the establishment of his 'consensus model of democracy'.

While the downward spiral evidently reached its peak in 2012, it had nevertheless been underway for several years, even for decades in the eyes of the most pessimistic observers. This leads to two questions in particular: how did the political situation degenerate so quickly? And, more important, why had northern Mali become a hotbed for rebellions and criminal activities?

Amadou Toumani Touré: a scapegoat for the 2012 crisis?

In answer to both questions, Amadou Toumani Touré is consistently presented as the chief, even unique, culprit for all Malian mistakes or failures. He undoubtedly contributed significantly to the political weaknesses and worsening security threats that plagued the country, but there is also no doubt that Mali's north-south relationships had been strained for several decades, and for some time before ATT took office in 2002. Unemployment, poverty, systemic inequalities, geographic isolation and lack of political representativeness indeed appeared to be as, if not more, important as ATT's failures in explaining the 2012 crisis. Since Mali became independent in 1960, territorial unity has been questioned and distrust between northern and southern communities has risen. Lack of goodwill on both sides, foreign spoiling influences and Bamako's game of divide and rule have contributed to heightened tensions between communities.

While these tensions have existed for decades, ATT's 10-year regime contributed, first, to fostering the gap between Mali's public image and the political reality, and second, to speeding the collapse of this democratic façade. By perverting local traditions of political dialogue for electoral purposes, or buying social and community peace with dangerous security compromises, President Touré fed his own weaknesses and fundamentally endangered Malian stability.

The Malian regime had been unable to address the issues that weakened national unity for decades or to create the conditions for an homogenous development of the country. It had also favoured community divisions in order to strengthen its power. As a result, ATT's trademark 'wait-and-see' approach in political, security and religious matters encouraged what were already established trends: namely, the emergence and development of areas free of state presence, and even the control of entire regions or strategic axes by groups involved in illicit or criminal activities that exerted a kind of para-sovereignty. ATT's rule also deepened Malian's dependence on foreign or neighbouring countries' assistance, and sometimes their political interference. The roles of Algeria and Libya in northern Mali have been highlighted several times, and it appears that the Malian authorities had become unable to control or regulate those exogenous influences. Conjecture as to the fate of promising northern natural resources, and to foreigners' economic prospects (including those of the Algerian public company SONATRACH for instance), also contributed to straining national relationships between north and south.

Furthermore, regular droughts or food crises in northern regions drove the development of foreign NGO activities. The particular permissiveness of ATT's regime to some of these

NGOs, especially regarding their Islamic-related activities (preaching, training of the Imam, Madrasas financing, etc) illustrated how the drift to foreign dependence had already worn down Mali's formal sovereignty, only for the presidency of ATT to make matters considerably worse.

When the Malian political regime collapsed in March 2012, after a successful but improvised mutiny of middle-class officers, Mali effectively revealed its 'institutional nudity' and the political fraud that the international community believed or pretended to believe in for years – and even, in some cases, helped to build.

Structure of the paper

Considering the work that has already been carried out in an effort to describe in detail the events of 2012, and to identify the immediate factors causing the conflict, this report is dedicated to discussing the root causes of the conflict. In so doing, it addresses the long-run trends that were accentuated under ATT, and eventually manifested in the sudden collapse of state control in the north and democratic continuity in the south.

Chapter 1 explores the dynamics of the state-building process in Mali and the long-term opposition between Bamako's authorities (and southern populations in general) and the Tuareg and Arab nomadic groups. It gives an overview of the main historical factors accounting for the tensions between communities, and explains how frustration and distrust have shaped 'north-south' relationships since the independence of Mali in 1960. Chapter 2 analyses the violence that accompanied the post-colonial process and the progressive establishment of a growing security threat in the north, which was met with a series of ineffective Malian responses. Bamako's conflictual relationships with the nomadic groups and the political authorities' repressive approach towards the 'northern issue' contributed to fostering the gap between north and south, and to opening the door to foreign interference. The presence of AQIM in the north, the extreme porosity of the Algerian border and the return of 'Libyan' fighters after Qaddafi's fall are among the main factors that have led to the 2012 crisis, and which are hallmarks of this hollowing out of official state control and its substitution by foreign influence. Chapter 3 details these factors, and highlights the regional and international interferences that have helped to foster the crisis. It discusses the massive security cooperation between Mali and Western countries and analyses the unexpected consequences of counter-terrorist programmes on global stability.

By describing the dynamics that have led, at sub-national, national, regional and international levels, to the 2012 crisis, this report aims to identify the foundations of what would be a viable, long-term plan for peace and security in Mali. It also serves as a one of the starting points for the new Maghreb-Sahel research programme which the Clingendael Institute's Conflict Research Unit has launched, with the support of the Dutch National Postcode Lottery.

Chapter One

A division to national unity, as it failed.

The events of 2012 were the most recent illustration of long-standing tensions between the southern and northern parts of Mali. With independence and the end of French colonial rule came the need for new Malian political elites to assert their authority over the whole territory. However, the approach taken at that time not only exacerbated tensions between government and northerners, but also led to the gradual political and economic marginalisation of the north. This withdrawal of the central state from a region once seen as prosperous and valuable turned northern Mali into a liability, and a security threat for the whole region.

The purpose of this chapter is to uncover the different elements that led to southern elites domination over northern Malian, and the construction of a radical opposition between north and the Malian authorities. It analyses the historical fault lines that preceded feelings of resentment among northern communities, the policies implemented by the central government that led populations in the north to turn on the state, and the foreign influences that aggravated an already explosive situation.

The dominance of the south in the aftermath of decolonisation

The Tuareg uprising of 2012 revealed an insurmountable tension between the north and south of Mali. This resentment can be partly traced back to methods of state formation in the immediate aftermath of decolonisation, which promoted aggressive unity and the constant marginalisation, in economic and political terms, of the north.

Despite past political unity (including the Soundjata Keïta Epic and history of the Malian Empire from the 13th century), relationships between north and south populations have always been distrustful. The French occupation even exacerbated these resentment. This is due to the attitude of the French during the colonial period, when they decided to educate a ruling class almost exclusively composed of majority black southerners. When these new ruling elites decided to free themselves from the colonial rule, they had to find a way to assert political authority over the whole Malian territory, and used strategies to do so that ranged from favouritism and patronage to economic marginalisation, divide-and-rule strategies and military control. This was far from helpful in strengthening the country's unity and popular adherence to the construction of a nation. In fact, by establishing an independent centralised state, based on the political and economic subordination of the north, the post-colonial elites laid the foundations for northern rebellions and future state failure. This chapter discusses how historical fault lines between the north and the south have shaped these dynamics.

Historical fault lines between the north and the south

While northern Mali is now seen by Malian authorities as a problem rather than a valuable part of the country, it has not always been that way. At times of trans-Saharan trades and royal pilgrimages to Mecca, northern regions were considered as key elements in the economic prosperity and political power of Mali. Northern Mali was an area of exploitation, commercial trade and a meeting point between Arab, Saharan and African worlds. Timbuktu, for instance, was a powerful commercial metropolis where gold was exchanged, negotiated and sold to countries in the Maghreb, Mashreq, Europe and the Mediterranean gulf. North Mali also had the monopoly over the extraction of salt, a commodity then seen as princely.

The end of the Malian great empires and French colonisation preceded the exclusion of northern regions from the centre of power. When the Malian government decided to abandon the Common Organisation of the Saharan Regions (OCRS) project in 1963, only five years after its inception, in order to avoid obstacles to its nation-building objectives, if fed a strong political resistance to the growing southern influence. Until then, OCRS membership had served as a counterweight to the rising political and territorial domination of the southern-dominated Malian state over the traditional nomadic areas that the Tuareg regarded as their own. Mali's exit from the OCRS fed a strong conviction among the Tuareg of northern Mali that they had been abandoned by the south.

The decision to marginalise the north after independence, which has been illustrated by the will of the central state to affirm its territorial integrity all over the country, added to the historical bias between northerners and southerners. Southern populations, indeed, have a profoundly negative perception of the north. The Tuareg are historically associated with insecurity because of their long and mythicised experience of 'rezzou', or raiding, against sedentary people. Other northerners, especially the Fulani or the Songhay people, have been the regular victims of these attacks. It partly explains the support of those communities for Malian independence and the authority of Bamako. The role of some northern nomadic groups in the trans-Saharan slave trade also helps to explain the historic and long-standing distrust between north and south.

Since 1960, the Tuareg and the Arab populations have never succeeded in fitting within the new Malian state model and have been regularly marginalised from positions of power and the central 'national cake'. Northern populations did not directly benefit from development programmes (unlike the south to a certain extent), nor did they succeed in securing access to the state's rent (due to very limited representation in parliament and government). This unequal access to state resources can be seen as the result of a divide-and-rule strategy implemented by the Malian government, which reached its peak under the ATT regime.

Divide-and-rule strategies

Beyond the political and economic marginalisation of northern populations, southern authorities kept trying to divide northern communities in order to prevent one group from gaining too much political influence and to ensure a weakened north. Electoral zoning constituted, for example, an important resource for the authorities in Bamako in terms of political representation of northern communities. By deciding to increase representation of the less densely populated regions, the Malian government gave the Tuareg communities, mainly living in deserted areas, an electoral advantage over the Arabs, who are generally considered to be even 'less Malian' than the Tuaregs, especially because of the privileged links they were supposed to have with other Arab-speaking countries (Mauritania, Algeria, Libya). It allowed them not only to favour the Tuareg over the Arabs, but also to favour certain groups within the Tuareg community. The underlying idea was to 'reward' those Tuareg communities that were the most hostile vis-à-vis the French coloniser and those that immediately supported the post-colonial regime. The Tuareg Iwellemmedan, for instance, a group spread in several northern districts, was more represented than the Tuareg Ifoghas ruling class, concentrated in the Adrar and supposed to have collaborated with the colonial settlers. But overall, the exercise of power largely remained the prerogative of southern elites, who made the rules and controlled the administration. When the 2012 crisis erupted, out of 147 deputies, only 12 Tuaregs were elected to the National Assembly while not a single representative of the Arab community (about 5 percent of the total population) occupied a seat. Since the last legislative elections in 2013, Zahabi Ould Sidi Mohamed is the first (and only) Arab representative to be elected for a position at the National Assembly.

On a security level, Bamako's government has also tried to undermine northern power by using the deep divisions within communities and by actively supporting anti-Tuareg vigilantes. Tuareg and Songhay militias (Ganda Koy or Ganda Iso, and today the Tuareg Imghad and Allies Self-defense Group (Groupe d'auto-défense Touareg Imghad et allies GATIA movement), which have been financed and equipped by the Malian government, are a good illustration of Mali's counter-insurgency tactics. These northern proxy combatants provided Bamako with an efficient tool to fight the Tuareg separatist movements and exacerbate tensions with northerners. Moreover, they gave the Malian authorities the opportunity to portray the northern region mainly as a security problem, and thereby to legitimate their own military approach to the situation.

Favouritism and patronage: Bamako's appointment logic

While political dialogue and national consensus are said to have been part of the Malian political culture since the 13th century (Soundjata Keita's political myth mainly), the post-colonial period has been exclusively dominated by southern political and military elites, who have known each other for a long time and are used to working together, having enjoyed the same schools, the same clandestine anti-colonial or democratic associations, and the same political influences and international networks (Pan African movements, Internationale Socialiste). This southern microcosm has been the main actor in the construction of the post-colonial state in Mali. Since independence, this solidarity-based group ran Mali for its own corporate interests, feeding a southern nationalism when it was politically necessary but without clearly addressing, at the same time, issues affecting south Mali communities (lack of economic development, high rate of corruption, very low generational turnover, etc). One cannot then consider an homogeneous and privileged south fighting against Tuareg or Arab irredentism but, more specifically, a central political society fighting for its own interests and using the southern nationalistic ground for consolidating its control over the Malian state.

In its own self-interest, Bamako implemented gestures of openness and reconciliation towards northern populations through the integration of northern elites into the state apparatus. However, these symbolic measures remained mostly focused on the need of the central state to use influential northern elites to 'manage' problems in the north. They also followed the strategic objectives of Bamako leaders, who sought to instrumentalise local divisions between communities in order to assert their power. These symbolic nominations, and strategies of buying northern support, were never aimed at increasing the national adhesion of the northern population to the Malian state. On the contrary, while these co-option strategies generally aimed at strengthening the presence of the central state in the peripheral regions, they also contributed to de-legitimating some northern 'collaborators' and exacerbating tensions between groups. In the end, Arab and Tuareg populations remained largely excluded from political power and, as a consequence, from rent-sharing circuits (even if local embezzlement strategies allowed some connected northern circles to be indirectly part of those circuits).

On top of these patronage tactics, Malian authorities also tried to unilaterally assert their presence all over national territory, and especially the north, by appointing loyal (i.e., southern) civil and military servants (préfets, governors). Most of the time, these appointments were seen as a 'punishment' for southern officials who always considered the northern region to be a hostile place and, somehow, a means for Bamako to keep them away from the centre. Some of them, belonging to the Malian military, were designated as governors of the northern regions.

Southern representatives sent to the northern regions then acted, most of the time, as if they were in a war or an occupied zone, with distrust and sometimes violence (several accusation of forced marriages, violence or humiliation of elders). This policy greatly contributed to a deep discontent among Arab and Tuareg populations, who interpreted it as a second colonisation and never accepted this legal authority. By unilaterally setting out the terms and conditions of its institutional presence in the northern regions, the Bamako government directly paved the way for local contestation and resentment. Moreover, through discretionary appointments of some northern actors to official functions, without prior consultation with local communities or consideration of regional fragile balances, the Malian government only exacerbated tensions within northern populations. These measures played a big role in damaging relations between the north and the southern political society –

fostering episodes of violence that have punctuated Malian history since independence.

The primacy of military means to enforce national unity

This perception, and the tendency of the Malian government to militarily administrate northern regions, has been very apparent since independence. It started in 1963 with the decision to place the north under martial law, and has continued recently with the appointment of Colonel Adama Kamissoko (a military senior ranking official) as the governor of Kidal after the 2012 rebellion.

The first post-colonial rebellion in 1963 can be seen as the direct consequence of this 'movement of local affirmation' that encouraged some Tuareg to use the momentum of political independence for their own separatist objectives. Despite several programmes aimed at reinforcing national unity and the legitimacy of the Bamako government within the northern region, north-south relations always remained overtly distrustful. The military coup in 1968 by General Moussa Traoré, and the establishment of a 30-year praetorian and centralised regime in Bamako (until the revolution of the 26 March 1991), did nothing to improve that.

Bamako's 'military' approach to the northern issue has been seen as one of the major components of the 2012 crisis. The embezzlement of funds allocated to the Special Programme for Peace, Security and Development in northern Mali (PSPSDN in French) in order to construct military barracks in northern regions is a good illustration of this military pattern. Using money that was supposed to be spent on local economic and social development, Mali's government decided to rebuild and re-equip its military infrastructure in the north. Local populations, hoping for social and development improvements, were greatly disappointed and saw this as another failure of state policy in the north.

By deliberately setting aside the economic and social dimensions of the repeated northern conflicts and mainly giving priority to repressive actions, Malian authorities paved the way for other non-national allegiances and foreign interferences.

Bypassing the Malian state: foreign aid and religious influences

Because of its geographic location, the north of Mali has always been a meeting point for foreign influences and for cultural, economic and religious connections. A constant lack of interest on the part of the Malian authorities, associated with post-colonial longing for a mythologised Tuareg state, have encouraged local populations to welcome and support some neighbouring countries' interference. Over time, northern Mali even became a central location in the competition for regional leadership, especially between Libya and Algeria, the two most active 'players' in the region over the past 30 years. These countries have been sometimes accused of supporting the rebels (Libya), or using this geographic area to contain insecurity outside their own borders (Algeria).

On top of these foreign state influences, north Mali also attracted foreign charity organisations, who officially assisted local populations with humanitarian aid. It is indeed true that these organisations generally helped northern populations to handle the weaknesses of the Malian state in terms of publics services and goods. Islamic NGOs, for instance, fulfilled an important social role among northern populations; in the absence of any economic perspectives and the withdrawal of the state, they provided education, health services and water supply to local communities. However, some of these organisations, supported by foreign countries (Saudi Arabia, Qatar, UAE, Libya, Kuwait), were accused of combining their charity activities with religious programmes and preaching, or with illicit trade. As a consequence, and despite their positive effect on northern populations, the real intentions of these NGOs were often questioned.

One of the most revealing examples of such alternatives to public systems of provision is that of the Madrasas. These religious schools rapidly became popular in Mali, and by the end of the 1980s, 25 percent of primary-age school children were attending these types of institution. Offering free education, the Madrasa enabled lower-class people to send their children to school, as it presented an alternative to the ineffective public education system and private schooling networks. But it also meant that the education was provided mostly in Arabic (in an area where colonial schools were not the norm, except for selected traditional leaders' sons, and use of French language was not common) and, therefore, created an additional gap between northern and southern populations.

Because of the inability of the Malian state to assert its authority on the whole territory, the northern regions were progressively controlled, or at least influenced, by foreign sponsors that sometimes directly contributed to questioning Malian unity. The historic position of the north in connecting the Maghreb and Mashreq regions with the rest of the country has progressively made those regions subject to suspicion, especially regarding religious influence and an alleged spread of radicalism.

As a result, while northern Mali was seen as the natural 'front door' for religious connections for centuries (with Maghreb and Middle East countries), it has been progressively suspected of becoming a playground for foreign religious influences and Islamic radicalism. Middle Eastern

NGOs, religious and charity organisations and Islamic organisations have flourished in the north of the country in the context of State weakness in deserted regions, importing Arab-speaking Imams and developing radical Islamic discourses that have been worrying central authorities and their Western partners.

Moreover, the diffusion of Wahhabism and the Tabligh Jamaat doctrine in Mali since the 1990s has also played a role in Bamako's suspicion regarding the north. The increasing influence of Saudi and Pakistani preachers and the growing popularity of the Tabligh proselytising organisations among northern populations, especially within the ranks of former Tuareg rebels, has worried Malian authorities and other foreign intelligence services. Despite a significant loss of influence since the 9/11 terrorist attacks, the Tabligh Jamaat still constitutes a strong religious reference among Tuaregs of the Ifoghas tribe. The radicalisation of Iyad ag Ghali, one of the main leaders of Tuareg rebellions since the 1990s, and the conversion of some Tuareg traditional leaders (e.g., the son of the recently deceased Ifoghas traditional leader Amenokal Intallah), are the most significant illustrations of the creeping influence of the movement within Tuareg communities. This alleged radicalism was used by Bamako to legitimate its repressive posture towards the north and to justify the 'martial' regime it imposed on these regions for decades.

In addition to other issues and mistrust that have historically contributed to the country's division into two separate entities, the alleged responsibility of northern tribes for the diffusion of radical Islamic doctrine has been seen as a direct threat by southern populations used to a tradition of religious tolerance and Islamic syncretism.

Divisions between north and south led not only to mutual distrust between communities but also to the intentional marginalisation of the north and the south's economic domination over it. The south imposing itself as the main centre of economic and political life led to growing discontent among northern populations and their continual feeling of distance from Bamako.

Economic inequalities between north and south

Northern regions have played a great role in what is now considered Mali, through their historical influence and economic prosperity. At the time of the great empires (from the 11th to the 16th century), the northern cities of Timbuktu (100,000 habitants in the 15th century, 54,000 now) or Gao (70,000 habitants in the 14th century, 50,000 in 1998, 80,000 now) were the most influential places in Mali, gathering political power and economic domination. After the Moroccan occupation (16th and 17th centuries), the territorial fragmentation of Mali (into local kingdoms and the Hausa 'cités-Etats') helped to shift the political centre of gravity towards the southern regions. With French colonial domination (1880/1890-1960), the centre of gravity moved towards the south and relegated the north of Mali to a position of secondary importance.

By becoming a political periphery, the northern regions lost their influence and directly suffered the domination of a 'foreign' south. Marginalised from power, they were also mostly excluded from economic programmes and nascent development, before being regarded as a hotspot of insecurity and a danger to regional stability. Due to the lack of regional official figures or local northern statistics (especially over lengthy time periods), this section mainly focuses on the economic trends and global disparities that have fed frustration and motivated some of the most violent uprisings. Where statistics exist, they are noted and interpreted to help explain the 2012 crisis and to highlight Mali's internal differences.

North Mali: from economic asset to liability

Despite common perceptions, the northern regions used to represent a major component of Mali's wealth and played an important role in the country's regional influence. However, the strategic reversal that led Bamako to assert its political and economic domination provoked a long-term break between north and south. Difficulties in endogenous development (including technical and security obstacles to exploitation of natural resources), the interference of foreign countries and the general weakness of the Malian state ultimately favoured the economic interests of the south. The end result was that the north turned into a barren economic zone plagued by insecurity and lacking any kind of infrastructure that could have enabled the development of a functioning economy. The south, on the other hand, could rely on a relatively well-functioning economy thanks to agriculture, gold mining and constant attention from the international community.

While northern regions are largely dependent on livestock and agriculture (42.7 percent of GDP) and tourism, the south relies mainly on gold mines (7.6 percent of the GDP and 75 percent of Mali's export revenue) and the exploitation of cotton (1 percent of the GDP) to fuel its economic activity. This geographic distribution of economic sectors makes the north more vulnerable to exogenous shocks. For instance, droughts in the 1970s and 1980s, or food crises in 2005, 2010 and 2012 have heavily affected northern populations, who are dependent on cereal purchases and self-production in their total consumption mix.

Regional crises have also weakened the northern economy, especially with regard to the exportation of livestock.

The growing insecurity in the north of Mali, especially after the first hostage takings in 2003 (when 32 Europeans were captured by the Group for Preaching and Combat (GSPC)), has also served to isolate the northern regions and aggravate the economic crisis. Tourism used to represent more than 80 billion FCFA of income (121 M€, only 1.2 percent of national GDP but one of the main sources of income for northern regions, where tourism sites are located) and provided jobs for 17,000 people in 2005. However, more than 8,000 people lost their jobs between 2009 and 2011, and the revenue generated by the sector dropped by 50 billion FCFA (76.2 M€). The continuous presence in the north of the GSPC, whose members converted into Al Qaeda in the Islamic Maghreb (AQIM) in 2007, has discouraged all tourist activities. The cancellation of world-renowned events such as the Paris-Dakar in 2008, the relocation of the Tuareg music Festival du Désert from 2003 to 2009, and the increase in travel warnings, has contributed to a further economic isolation of the north.

On top of that, unemployment and poverty have created generational imbalances and frustration for younger people in particular. While this is an often under-researched area, because of the lack of data available, it is important to bear in mind that a growing demography can further aggravate the economic situation of Mali and foster tensions in the future. Young people indeed make up more than 50 percent of the population and do not feel well represented by political, traditional or religious leaders. The lack of job opportunities for them and the low turnover in leadership positions has led to the breakdown of a contract between the cadets sociaux and the elders. Young people have become frustrated by the difficulties of improving their social status, as they see their chances of finding a job or getting married fade away. This situation has fostered a generation of disillusioned young people.

From local liability to regional security threat

The structural weaknesses of the northern economy and its vulnerability to shocks have often pushed nomadic populations, such as Tuareg and Arab tribes, beyond Mali's borders. These economic and climatic refugees made temporary settlements in neighbouring countries, for example Niger, Algeria, Burkina Faso or Mauritania, but their arrival also created tensions with local communities, such as disputes over land and over access to water and pastures. In Libya, male refugees were integrated into Qaddafi's Islamic Legion and took part in several wars which the Libyan regime was involved in (e.g., the 1978-

1987 war in Chad). These exiled Tuareg combatants would later constitute the hardcore of northern Mali rebellions, especially those of the 1990s.

With its 1,316km border with northern Mali, Algeria has became an emigration destination for northern populations. Commercial ties between the north of Mali and the south of Algeria have developed over the years. For decades, Malian traders and seasonal workers crossed the Algerian border, looking for economic opportunities. In fact, Algeria and Mali institutionalised this free movement of migrants through bilateral agreements, in order to give a legal framework to this 'barter economy'. But in the 1990s, at a time of great instability in Algeria, suspicious trades (such as arms, contraband and drugs) started to mingle with this legitimate free movement of good and people. Criminal groups and terrorist organisations thrived on illegal trades. Mokhtar

Belmokhtar, for instance, the commander of one the GSPC's main katiba, made a name for himself (he is now known as Mr Marlboro) by smuggling cigarettes through the northern Mali/southern Algeria border.

The limited economic opportunities and the geographic location of northern Mali have made it a hub for trafficking. The criminal economy that emerged in the 1980s attracted more and more young people as it intensified and diversified. Drugs, cigarettes, illegal immigration flows, counterfeit products and stolen car parts were exchanged between the Sahel's populations. The passivity and sometimes collusion at the highest level of the Malian state allowed this illicit economy to prosper. The example of 'Air Cocaine' in 2009 is revealing, as it triggered world-wide suspicion of the Malian state; the fact that a plane of this size was able to land in this region raised questions about the involvement of state officials.

Rampant corruption also presents a challenge for any economic recovery for the north. While the region contains resources that could potentially benefit the population if exploited effectively, the short-term perspective adopted by the authorities, coupled with prospects for personal gains, seriously undermine this opportunity.

Deliberate underdevelopment of the northern region

Northern Mali is thought to be very promising in terms of energy and mineral resources. According to a study conducted by the Authority for Oil Research (Autorité pour la recherche pétrolière, AUREP), a service created by the Malian government in 2005 and attached to Secretariat General of the Ministry of Mines, the subsoil of Kidal, Gao and Timbuktu could contain around 850,000km^2 of oil and gas. Four main basins have been identified: Taoudeni (in the borderland of Mali, Algeria and Mauritania), Tamensa (halfway between Mali and Niger), the 'graben de Gao' and the 'rift de Nara' (close to Mopti). The Algerian national company SONATRACH has already made massive investments in the Taoudenit field for prospect operations (alleged $60 million). After operations were suspended during the 2012 crisis, Algeria asked for a quick restart of its activities in northern Mali. Furthermore, there is uranium in the north of Mali, as shown by the potential 200 tonnes available in the Samit deposit in the Gao region.

These findings are encouraging with regards to the future economic vitality of the northern regions and could be a sign to central government that it should work on the economic development of the north. However, the AUREP study seems designed only to attract foreign investors, and indicates that the north should be divided into several 'blocks' (most of the licences have already been sold to foreign companies such as SONATRACH).

Moreover, Bamako has not so far shown any will to involve northern populations in those projects (fearing that mining income will create new separatist tensions), nor has it any plans to link these economic opportunities to the development of essential local infrastructure. Worst of all, northern natural resources could encourage new tensions between north and south, and contribute to new cycles of violence. For some southerners, the exploitation of natural resources would hence constitute a major threat to Malian national unity as it would fuel economic competition between the different communities, each trying to gain a 'slice of the cake'.

Conclusion

Economic inequalities and unequal political representation have fed historical resentment against the state, especially among northern Malian communities, for decades. Experienced as a double marginalisation by northern populations, they partly explain the permanent disagreements with Bamako, and played a huge role in rebellions that have occurred since independence in 1960.

From the Tuareg side, the establishment of Bamako as the capital of a new state they never wanted to be a part of, has never met local expectations. From the Bamako side, the deserted regions have long been seen as highly dangerous, no-go areas. The southern military have never been trained or well equipped to fight against rebels, who are well organised, have very mobile units and perfectly control their environment.

Since 1963, however, Malian authorities have often preferred to use a military option to address northern crises. Martial law, military governors, and the building of new barracks and garrisons have always constituted a permanent (and the most symbolic) component of conflict and post-conflict management frameworks.

By deliberately setting aside the economic and political dimensions of discontent, Bamako indirectly gave some groups and northern leaders the grounds on which they could mobilise parts of the local population against the central state. Except for the 1963 post-independence movement, the three other rebellions that Mali has experienced (in 1990, 2006 and 2012) were all founded on political and economic claims.

Chapter Two

Destruction in northern Mali, Rebellion outbrake.

Historical lack of understanding and mutual distrust between Bamako and its northern territory have played an important role in Malian instability for decades. By ignoring northern aspirations for economic development (especially social and economic infrastructure) or political representation (lack of governmental seats for instance), the Malian authorities have paved the way for violent contestation and separatist actions. The popular support among Tuareg and Arab populations for some rebel movements and armed groups, and the authority the rebel leaders have had over some northern populations, are good illustrations of the inequalities collectively experienced by the northern population.

The subsequent rebellions in Mali have, in turn, aggravated the long-standing community distrust. The aftermath of the rebellions and the negotiations that led to 'peace agreements' also fostered tensions among northern communities, as some groups used those situations to advance their own interests.

The ethnic divisions and lawlessness, due to the withdrawal of the Malian state, that characterised the aftermath of rebellions presented a window of opportunity for terrorist groups to settle in the north. Thriving on illicit trafficking and mixing with local populations, these groups managed to gradually gain influence before the 2012 crisis.

This chapter explains the security issues created by tensions within Malian society, and describes how the central government tried to address them.

Constant rebellion: the historical continuity of Tuareg anger

From 1960 to 2012, there were four Tuareg rebellions and five different (and so far ineffective) north-south peace agreements.

Despite these peace agreements, disarmament programmes and other foreign economic sponsorships (from Algeria and Libya, but also from Western countries), the Malian central state has been accused of marginalising the northern regions and, as a consequence, north-south relations remain tense. By repressing the rebels or buying a precarious peace (e.g., co-opting rebel leaders), Malian authorities tended to set aside the real – political and economic – roots of the conflict. Moreover, by giving to some rebel leaders a disproportionate influence in the negotiating processes (Iyad ag Ghali for instance), Bamako altered the nature of the conflict and fed divisions within the northern groups.

Historical tensions between north and south have always played a decisive role in the cycles of rebellion, although other factors have also fed resentment and helped to perpetuate the conflict. The peace agreements and economic incentives given to some combatants in order to disarm them have indirectly encouraged, in a depressed economic environment, a rebel economy and the emergence of local entrepreneurs of violence. Foreign interference and the central position of northern Mali in the regional race for Sahelian leadership have also influenced the conflict. By actively sponsoring the rebels or indulging them through cross-border movements or supplies, some neighbouring countries (especially Libya and Algeria) have played a big role in destabilising the region and locking the parties into permanent tensions.

This section recounts the rebellions that have taken place in northern Mali since independence in 1960. It describes local and regional responses, including the various peace treaties and pacts that have been signed, and the global consequences they have had on Malian stability up until today.

1963-1991: post-colonial rebellions and Bamako's military responses

Occurring only three years after independence, the first rebellion in 1963 demonstrated the difficulties of addressing post-colonial challenges and gathering all Malian communities within a single political entity. The choice made by the Malian post-colonial authorities to repress the rebellion, and their refusal to address the root causes of the crisis (i.e., political recognition of northern specificities and a special status for the region), helped to sustain the conflict for years. The authorities' decision to forbid tourism and establish martial law and military administration in the northern regions illustrated the approach taken to address northern issues.

The overthrow of President Modibo Keita in 1968 and the establishment of General Moussa Traoré military regime helped to quell public discontent, at least for a couple of years and on the surface. However, severe droughts in 1972-1973 and in 1984-1985 fed new discontent by pushing thousands of members of northern tribes to leave the region and seek refuge in neighbouring countries, especially Niger and, to some extent, Libya. If those exiles did not directly destabilise the Malian regime, the exodus led to frustration, distrust and discontent among the northern population. It also encouraged new connections with other groups, especially in Niger, where Tuareg rebel movements had also been active since independence. The Libyan regime 'warmly' welcomed those climate-driven refugees as the Jamahiriya leader, Muammar Qaddafi, saw them as a way to assert his political influence in the Sahara. Integrated within the Libyan Islamic legion (created in 1972), Tuaregs were militarily trained and equipped and took part in wars that the Libyan regime led by proxy in other African countries, especially in Chad.

Tuareg and Arab exiles were the main participants in the 1990-1991 second rebellion. Like their elders before them, combatants fought for better living conditions and the recognition of a northern political identity, but also asked that Tuareg be allowed to be combatants in the Malian national army. By deciding to ignore the political motivation of the rebels and preferring to call them 'highway thugs', General Moussa Traoré repeated Modibo Keita's mistakes and contributed, once again, to the radicalisation of the movement.

Abuses, especially from the Malian military in the regions of Gao, Kidal and Menaka, aggravated the grievances of the north. Because of its knowledge of the region and the suspected connivance between the rebels and the Libyan regime, Algeria was chosen by the Malian regime as the mediator of the crisis. However, the Tamanrasset peace agreements that were signed on 6 January 1991 were called into question by the overthrow of General Moussa Traoré on 26 March, after a popular revolution of democratic clandestine organisations and the army, led by Lieutenant-Colonel Amadou Toumani Toure.

'Post-democratic' rebellions and community divisions in the north

The 26 March 1991 democratic revolution put an end to 30 years of the Union pour la démocratie et le peuple malien (UDPM) single-party regime. Despite those political changes, the security situation in the north did not improve and divisions grew within the armed groups themselves, especially between the Ifoghas (led by Iyad ag Ghali) and the non-Ifoghas tribes (Tuareg and Arabs). With the help of Algeria, Mauritania and France, the new Malian political authorities, with the coordination of the armed groups, agreed the Pacte National. Signed in Bamako on 11 April 1992, the Pacte intended to redefine national relationships between north and south according to several main principles: a significant military withdrawal from the northern regions, a massive integration of the rebels into the Malian army, greater territorial political autonomy (with the creation of elected local assemblies holding sovereign powers in the economic and the security fields), and an ambitious development programme. In exchange, Tuareg agreed to give up their political claims regarding the independence of Azawad.

Despite this symbolic show of willingness to address the issues that provoked the crisis and the inequalities between north and south, the new Malian regime did not succeed in gathering all the northern tribes around its project. New waves of tension arose due to deep divisions among the Tuareg populations, both historical and political, the questioned leadership of Iyad ag Ghali, and the slow pace of political and economic reform. In 1996, after four years of uneasy peace, the parties involved signed the Timbuktu peace agreement and commemorated a Cérémonie des flammes de la paix, supposedly ending the war and initiating a fresh start.

But a succession of crises in the north, alleged preferential treatment and fears of new military involvement fed continuous southern distrust regarding Malian's irredentist north. Meanwhile, people in the north continued to suffer from developmental inequalities and internal divisions.

The inability of the Malian government to implement the promises made in 1992 deepened national divisions and the rift between the northern and southern territories.

President Amadou Toumani Touré (ATT), elected in 2002, aggravated the gap between north and south and significantly raised the security threat in northern Mali. His mistakes undoubtedly paved the way to the 2012 crisis.

Tuareg rebellions under the ATT regime: disunity, interference and terrorism

After 10 years of fragile peace and mutual suspicion, a third rebellion broke out in May 2006. Once again led by Iyad ag Ghali, the combatants took advantage of the withdrawal of the Malian military in the north after the last peace agreement to take control of the cities of Kidal and Menaka. For the third time since 1992, Algeria offered to lead a mediation process. However, the peace agreement signed in July 2006 in Algiers was considered too favourable to Iyad ag Ghali's personal agenda. As a consequence, several Malian political parties (especially the Rassemblement pour le Mali headed by Ibrahim Boubacar Keita) and non-Ifoghas Tuareg leaders refused to endorse it. The Tuareg, indeed, considered Iyad's Ifoghas community to be the only beneficiaries of the agreement, while Bamako's political leaders rejected the compromises made by Amadou Toumani Touré towards the rebellion, believing that the problem had to be addressed militarily. For them, by negotiating with armed groups without even trying to stop the insurgency, ATT ignored what they saw as the main roots of the problems. Detractors accused him of striking a deal in order to prevent any delay in holding the 2007 presidential elections (which would compromise the prospect of his own re-election). Doubts regarding a possible collusion between

Iyad ag Ghali's movement and the AQIM terrorist organisation reinforced the criticism of ATT's weak management of security issues. Increasing rumours of alleged high-level complicity with traffickers and armed groups punctuated ATT's second term as head of the Malian state.

Despite the growing discontent of some northern groups regarding the advantages given to Iyad ag Ghali's supporters, ATT decided to ignore them and reinforce ag Ghali's position by feeding divisions within non-Ifoghas Tuareg communities. Two northern militias were set up by Bamako to fight against the new North Mali Tuareg Alliance for Change (ATNMC), an armed group led by Ibrahim ag Bahanga in opposition to Iyad ag Ghali's leadership. The first militia group was led by El Hadj Gamou, a Tuareg Imghad who nurtured an acrid hatred towards the Ifoghas community and gave allegiance to Bamako; the other group was composed of Tilemsi Arabs, whose leader,

Major Colonel Abderahmane Ould Meydou, later negotiated with Bamako the liberation of Mohamed Ould Aiwanatt, a very influential Arab businessman involved in the 'Air Cocaine' operation, in exchange for the support of his community. Bamako's divide- and-rule policy led to a 'tribalisation' of the northern conflict and to the rapid obsolescence of the Algiers agreement.

After Algeria, Libya volunteered to negotiate with ag Bahanga. A new peace settlement, the fifth agreement since the fall of the Malian military regime in 1991, was signed in October 2009, in Sebha (Libya). Tuareg rebels, along with Malian and Nigerien representatives, agreed to end the fighting, while the Libyan regime offered asylum to Bahanga to ensure his respect for the pact.

The aftermath of the Tuareg rebellions: state withdrawal and security vacuum

The partial implementation of clauses contained in the different peace agreements led to a withdrawal of the central state from the northern regions. The decentralisation promised by the agreements, even though it was badly implemented, led to a demilitarisation of the north and created what could be called a 'security vacuum' around the cities of Gao, Timbuktu and Kidal.

Combined with the lack of economic development in the north and the resentment of local populations against the state, the security vacuum in the north presented terrorist groups with an opportunity to settle. The GSPC, later called Al Qaeda in the Islamic Maghreb (AQIM), was the first group to enter northern Mali, in 2003. Because of its significant financial resources, collected through the kidnapping of Western tourists and its involvement in trafficking, the organisation was able to fill the void left by the state in the north. Buying the support of local criminal networks and the goodwill of the northern community by 'distributing money, handing out medicine, treating the sick and buying SIM cards', the GSPC acted as a social security provider in regions abandoned by the state. This enabled the organisation to conduct its activities without being bothered by the state and allowed it to attract young recruits, attracted by the prospect of easy money and disappointed by the lack of other local economic perspectives. MUJAO, which became active in Mali after its split with AQIM, in 2011, followed the same kind of pattern.

Overall, the decisions made after the Tuareg rebellions paved the way for terrorist groups in the sense that they could act as a para-sovereign organisation or 'substitute government' in the north in the absence of a strong central state. The lack of reaction, and sometimes the complicity of some Malian political leaders, allowed these groups to prosper and contributed markedly to the deterioration of the security situation in the north.

Northern disunity as a main cause of instability?

Beyond the undeniable lack of political will on both sides, the failure of the Malian national pact is also linked to internal divisions within northern communities and the continuous attempts from Bamako and the international community to address northern issues as a hegemonic bloc. North Mali is deeply divided into several communities, groups, clans and political leaderships that conform to distinct political 'myths and mythologies'. In order to achieve long-term stability, Malian authorities would have to deal with different interests and sometimes contradictory local demands.

Tuareg, Arab, Songhay or Fulani people have different political agendas, social or security claims. They do not share the same culture, languages or traditions; they do not all recognise Azawad as their common land and the need for independence as an end in itself. Those communities rarely fought for the same armed group nor were they sponsored by the same key player (Algeria and Libya for Arabs and Tuareg, Bamako for the Songhay, etc). If those differences and divisions are the biggest challenges for the Malian state to overcome on the path to peace, they are also the direct result of Bamako's policies towards those communities (i.e., government-sponsored militias in the north and Bamako's divide-and-rule tactics in the region).

Current difficulties in the Algiers peace talks are directly connected to those community divisions. The Platform and Coordination groups that are supposed to represent northern interests in the peace process do not have a common agenda, including on territorial matters (autonomy, federalism, decentralisation – among other issues). Those differences make it extremely difficult to agree on common discussion points and any viable solution to the crisis continues to be unattainable. Understanding the dynamics of northern groups is therefore crucial to achieving a long-term peace agreement and meeting local needs that are currently ignored or fulfilled by others, including terrorist organisations.

Origins and political allegiances of the northern communities

Northern Mali has a very low-density population, with just 1.3 million inhabitants (out of 14.5 million in Mali as a whole), and the communities who live there (Tuareg, Arab, Songhay or Fulani) are deeply divided. Tuareg and Arabs represent more than 60 percent of the Septentrion, with Tuareg groups forming a significant majority.

Those internal divisions have always seriously affected the unity of rebel movements and made it even more difficult to use a blueprint or pre-established framework to put an end to crises, including that in 2012.

While Tuareg are numerically predominant in the three northern regions (Timbuktu, Gao and Kidal), deep internal divisions have nevertheless prevented them from becoming indisputable leaders in the north. In creating the Mouvement national pour la liberation de l'Azawad (MNLA) in 2011, Ibrahim ag Bahanga aimed to unite all the Tuareg communities within a single organisation in order to avoid past mistakes and divisions that have undermined their influence. He succeeded until Iyad ag Ghali created his own organisation, Ansar Dine, in 2012 and actively recruited within the Tuareg Ifoghas. The fragile unity of northern movements did not survive this.

The next section analyses the dynamics of northern communities, especially the divisions within Tuareg and Arab tribes, which have weaken past rebellion movements and now complicate the resolution of the conflict. It also highlights the deep differences between these communities and other northern groups, especially the Fulani and the Songhay, who are historically closer to the Malian state and have sometimes been used by Bamako against the Tuareg rebels.

Tuareg communities: disunity within pluralism

Disunity, along with the lack of training and poor military equipment, have been some of the major weaknesses in past 'Tuareg' rebellions. Since the time of colonial domination of Sudan, disputes among communities, especially among the Tuareg, have been used to weaken any possible unity and impose 'exogenous' political orders. The very rigid social structure of the Tuareg community – with noble, vassal, religious or former serf clans – greatly facilitates divisive strategies.

Each Tuareg clan is divided into numerous groups and sub-clans, sometimes with different political agendas. The town of Kidal has no less than 60 Tuareg sub-groups, organised mainly into the 'noble' Ifoghas (four main sub-groups), the Taghat elet (two main sub-groups) and the Idnan (two sub-groups). Subordinate 'vassal' (Imghad) or 'former serf' clans (the Bella, a sedentary lower class whose members are regularly used as informal slaves) are also represented in the city even though they do not control the political or traditional power. After independence in 1960, the Ifogha were divided into pro- and anti-Bamako clans. Two Ifogha brothers, Intallah and Zaid ag Attaher disagreed on the clan's relationship with Bamako. Intallah eventually chose to support the new central state and was rewarded for his loyalty by being endorsed as the new Amenokal (traditional chieftaincy) of the Ifogha community. His relatives still run the community (the new Amenokal, Mohamed ag Intallah, created the High Council for the unity of Azawad, HCUA, a group involved in the current peace talks alongside the MNLA within the same Coordination).

In other Malian cities, especially Gao and Ménaka, Ifoghas are much less represented, contrary to the Idnan, Iwellemmedan and the Chaman-Amas. The Iwellemmedan, a noble cast of Tuareg pastoralists, have historically played a huge role in the region, especially during the colonial era when it led the 1914-1916 rebellions against the French army. They then represented the dominant Tuareg group in Mali before being supplanted by the Ifoghas, who were supported by the colonial administration because they were less hostile to foreign troops. After independence, the Iwellemmedan were electorally favoured by Bamako as a counter-influence the Ifoghas. The current leader of this community, Bajan ag Hamatou, is still serving as deputy of Ménaka.

Lastly, in the Timbuktu region, where the Songhay are numerous, Tuareg groups are mainly composed of Iwellemmedan and Kel Instar. The latter regard themselves as descending from Arabs and, as a consequence, have close ties with other Arab groups, especially the Bérabiche. Because of their historic 'rights' over the richest lands, the Kel Instar are very influential in Timbuktu. Kel Instar Zakyatou walette Halatine, a former Minister of Tourism in the ATT regime, had her home in Bamako totally damaged after the launching of the Tuareg rebellion in January 2012. This event confirmed the deep distrust between southern communities (mostly Bambaras) and Tuareg or Arab members.

The 1990s rebellion further divided the Tuareg community and highlighted tensions that still strongly shape northern communities. While fighters from the Kidal Ifogha ruling clan signed the Tamanrasset agreement in 1991, the Tamasheq lower class (Imghad) and the Tuareg from Timbuktu (Kel Instar) or Menaka (Chaman-Amas) split from Iyad ag Ghali's Mouvement pour l'Azawad (MPA). Mutual accusations of hogging the limelight in the negotiations or compromising with southerners, have weakened the Tuareg movements and allowed the Malian government to regain control of the events. Those divisions were also seen again in 2006, especially with the schism between ag Bahanga and Iyad ag Ghali. However, during the first months of the 2012 rebellion, the MNLA succeeded in representing all the clans of Tuareg society. But the creation of Ansar Dine put an end to this very temporary unity and led to new divisions – among the Tuareg (MNLA, Ansar Dine, Haut Conseil pour l'Unité de l'Azawad – HCUA, Front de Libération de l'Azawad – FPA, GATIA, etc), the Arabs (MAA, MUJAO, etc) and the Songhay

(Coordination des Mouvements et Fronts Patriotiques de Résistance – CM-FPR) especially.

The Arabs: revolt from the margins

While numerically inferior in northern Mali, Arab communities are far less divided than the Tuaregs. Composed only of three main groups, Arabs have been deeply marginalised by the Malian central power. Before the 2012 crisis, no Arab succeeded in being elected to the National Assembly or the High Council of Regional Authorities (HCCT). On the contrary, 12 Tuareg representatives (out of 147) and numerous Tuareg territorial councillors, including Iyad ag Ghali himself, have represented northern interests in Bamako. To compensate for this clear political inequity, in October 2007 Amadou Toumani Touré appointed Moctar El Moctar, an Arab from the Tilemsi, as Minister of Communication. In 2013, for the first time in Malian political history, an Arab, Mohamed Ould Sidi Mohamed was elected as Deputy of Goundam.

Living mainly in the Gao and Timbuktu regions, Arabs are divided between noble clans (Kounta), emancipated groups (Tilemsi Arab) and the Berabiche (most of them in Timbuktu). Kountas occasionally liaise between Ifoghas from Kidal and Berabiche from Timbuktu but have generally lost a great deal of their past dominant influence. Tilemsi Arabs are thought to be very influential in regional trafficking (especially the Lamhar tribe) and to have strong links with the MUJAO. Their influence in the Gao region is one factor that has explained the MUJAO control of this city in 2012. In the past, this clan was supported by the Malian government in order to facilitate negotiations with AQIM (on hostage release, ransom intermediaries).

The Berabiche are very influential in northern Mali, living in Timbuktu (around 35 different factions) and also in the region from the Mauritanian border to the north of the Kidal region. By securing convoys across the desert, they became a key element of the criminal economy in the whole region. Since 2006, and the failed attempt by Kountas to impose their leadership upon all the Arab tribes (Coordination des communautés arabes du Mali – CCAM), the relationships between Kountas and Berabiche are more distant. During the last crisis, Berabiche created the National Front for the Liberation of Azawad (FPLA) and the Arab Movement of Azawad (MAA).

Arab communities have actively participated in all the 'Tuareg' rebellions (by, for instance, contributing troops), at least until Malian political liberalisation in 1991. Indeed, from the signature of the Pacte national in 1991 to the last 2012 crisis, Arab communities fostered links with the Malian government, mainly to protect their trade interests. Currently, General Mohamed Abderhamane Ould Meydou, a Tilemsi Arab and a former rebel leader/military multi-deserter (in 1999 and 2004), is, for instance, one of the main Malian military staff involved in the north (he negotiated with Bamako the support of Tilemsis in exchange for the release of Mohamed Ould Aiwanatt).

While the positions, political allegiances or regional interests of each Tuareg or Arab group have differed historically, the political use of northern divisions by colonial and post-colonial actors (sometimes with a reversal of ancient social organisations) has also deeply complicated any understanding of northern dynamics. Those community divisions explain the growth of armed groups (especially within the Tuaregs) and, at the same time, help to explain the difficulty of implementing a viable solution to the crisis. They partly account for the failure of previous agreements and are significant factors in the current situation.

The Songhay and the Fulani

The disunity between northern populations has been deepened by Fulani (14 percent of the northern population) and Songhay (7 percent) resentment against the Tuareg and the Arabs. However, unlike Tuareg communities, these groups are far less divided and well more integrated with the central state. The two communities have played a major political role in Mali's history and have never accepted that Tuareg grievances were overshadowing their own needs. Their positions have been well understood by Bamako, which regularly used Tuareg divisions to weaken the rebel movements.

The Songhay have lived in northern Mali (especially in the Gao region) since the 9th century, and from 1325 to 1375, the Songhay city of Gao was politically incorporated into the Malian Empire. However, at the end of the 15th century, the Songhay Prince Sonni Ali expelled the Malian

Mandingoes from Gao and started to build what would become the Songhay Empire. After taking Timbuktu back from the Tuareg in 1468 and the commercial city of Djenné in 1473, the Songhay Empire developed and prospered. Politically centralised and held by a powerful aristocracy, the empire took an Islamic turn under the reign of Askia Mohammed (1493), the successor of Ali, who made a pilgrimage to Mecca and earned the title of 'Caliph of the Sudan'. After several wars of conquest in the name of Islam, the Songhay Empire reached its peak before being conquered by the Moroccans at the end of the 16th century.

The illustrious history of the Songhay and their significant contribution to Mali's prosperity and prestige help to explain their attachment to the territorial integrity of Mali and their good political relationships with the central state. The Songhay community is fully involved in Bamako's political life: Amadou Toumani Touré (former president),

Choguel Kokalla Maiga (government spokesman), Soumeylou Boubeye Maiga (former minister), Soumaila Cissé (former minister, former President of the Commission of the West African Monetary Union, current head of the political parliamentary opposition), all Songhay, have held high-level positions within the Malian political sphere.

The Fulanis' history in Mali started with their settling in Macina (a region corresponding to the inner Niger Delta) somewhere between the 7th and 9th century. From the 13th to the 19th century, the Fula people lived under the domination of the Empire of Mali (until the early 15th century), the Songhai Empire (mid-15th century) and the Segou kings (until 1818). At the end of the Segou reign, the Fulani, led by Hamadou Bari (later known as Cheikou Amadou), rebelled against southern Bambara clans. Capitalising on the massive conversion to Islam that had struck the Macina, Amadou succeeded in implementing a theocratic regime and creating the Macina Kingdom, called Dina (literally, the 'belief in Islam'). Organised around the Hamdallaye political centre, the Macina was also divided into five regions, each administrated by governors in charge of implementing sharia law and diffusing Islam from the top to the bottom of the kingdom. The Macina was prosperous when it was attacked and conquered by the jihadist leader, El Hadj Omar Tall, in 1862. The assault on the Macina was the result of the kingdom sheltering the Bambara Segou King, one of the main targets of Omar Tall's jihad. The domination of the Toucouleurs (1862-1890) and, later, the French (until 1960), did not interrupt the historic influence of the Fulani, as these two entities maintained the political organisation of the Dina.

Even in recent times, Fulani political leaders have played a very important role in Mali; for instance, Adame Ba Konaré (one of the most renowned

Malian historians and wife of former president Alpha Oumar Konaré), Oumar Tatam Ly (first prime minister of IBK) and Ali Nouhoum Diallo (the former president of the National Assembly) are all Fulani. Their presence in Malian political or intellectual fields illustrates the fact that some northern communities are included in central state structures, even they are numerically under-represented.

Bamako's northern militias: a proxy counter-insurgency strategy

Because of their past history and important role in Malian politics and the dissemination of Islam, the Songhay and Fulani became very critical of the continuous Tuareg uprisings. Not only did the Tuareg try to establish themselves as the 'voice of the north', articulating the grievances of every community in the northern regions, they also conducted regular attacks on Songhay and Fulani sedentary and semi-nomadic populations.

In the 1990s, during the second Tuareg rebellion, a Songhay self-defence militia, the Ganda Koy ('masters of the land'), was created to protect sedentary populations against bandits and lighter-skinned nomads (primarily Tuareg and Arabs, commonly referred to as 'the Whites'). At the time of its creation, this militia benefited from direct support from the Fulani, the Bozos ('people from the river'), and the Bellas (the Tuareg lower class) and from the indirect support of the Malian army. Soumeylou Boubeye Maiga, a Songhay (former head of the Malian intelligence service, former Minister of Foreign Affairs and first Minister of Defence after IBK's presidential election) is allegedly the main instigator of this vigilante initiative. The alleged support of the Malian state for the militias (e.g., handing out cash and arms) would have allowed state services to discreetly intervene in the conflict without formally engaging the army and suffering losses among southern military personnel. At the same time, it also helped to arouse the spectre of tribal war in the country.

The Ganda Koy conducted brutal attacks on Tuareg and Arab populations, giving an ethnic and racial component to the 1990s Malian crisis. The most 'famous' Ganda Koy operation involved the killing of 53 Mauritanians and Tuareg Marabouts of the Kel Essouk clan, near Gao in 1994. The militia was seen to be dissolved in 1996 during the Timbuktu 'Cérémonie des Flammes de la Paix'. However, the movement only entered a 'dormant phase' and was never officially dismantled. It has even been reactivated several times since then, especially when tensions within rival communities re-emerge. After the creation of the MNLA in 2011, the movement resurfaced and called on Songhay and Fulani military to join in order to counter the Tuareg fighters returning from Libya.

Parallel to Ganda Koy, another self-defence militia was created: the Ganda Iso. This group was created in 2009 by Seydou Cissé, one of the main figures of Ganda Koy. Cissé led the political branch and a Fulani, Sergeant Amadou Diallo, was appointed as the head of the military branch. However, Diallo's responsibility in the Hourala massacre of 2008 provoked tensions at the top of the movement, as he had committed a public massacre of four Tuareg civilians in the village on a market day. That atrocity triggered retaliations by the Tuareg and led to a split between the military and the political leadership of Ganda Iso. From that moment on, tensions between the Tuareg and Ganda Iso increased, leading to multiple battles.

During the 2012 crisis, Ganda Koy and Ganda Iso chose to collaborate with the Malian army against the Tuareg, especially in the Gao region. The two militias merged during the conflict and created the CM-FPR, in order to advance their interests during the peace talks with Algiers. Since June 2014, the

CM-FPR has been part of the 'Platform' (alongside one branch of the Arab Movement of the Azawad – MAA, and the Coordination for the People of Azawad – CPA). These groups are opposed to the 'Coordination' that gathers Tuareg and Arabs fighters from the MNLA, the HCUA, a group led by Mohamed ag Intallah and mainly composed of former Ansar Dine members, and the MAA.

Since the beginning of the Algiers peace talks in April 2014, Bamako has decided to support the GATIA, a Tuareg militia backed by the Malian army (and controlled by General ag Gamou), in order to fight the MNLA. On top of its use of Songhay and Fulani groups, Bamako further divided the northern 'front' by actively engaging Tuareg fighters against the rebels. In deciding to do so, the Malian government gave its implicit consent to a de facto 'tribalisation' of the conflict, which has had serious consequences for the security situation in the north and for current negotiations on a solution to the conflict.

Conclusion

The history of national and inter-community violence in Mali has accompanied the post-colonial state-building process. Since 1963, rebellions and other security crises have challenged Malian unity and the legitimacy of 'Bamako policy' in administrating the national territory. The diversity of the Malian population has been used as a divide-and-rule instrument, first by French colonists and then by post-colonial politicians, in order to assert their authority in the north, but also by the Tuareg noble class to impose its leadership upon the entire community.

All past peace agreements have failed, partly because of this disunity and the difficulty, in that context, of satisfying the interests of all communities (which would, in turn, guarantee a post-conflict stability). Because local interests differed, and were even sometimes incompatible, past agreements have not been able to sustain a viable peace between north and south and within the northern communities. Since independence, tensions and regular episodes of violence have deepened national antagonisms and fed southern resentment towards the 'armed bandits of the north'. The growth of illicit trafficking and criminal activities in the north also encouraged Bamako's historically 'tough' posture. Excessive militarisation of the problems in the north, the failure to address the economic dimension of the crisis, and discretionary benefits dispensed to a small number of affiliated or friendly clans, have exacerbated tensions. Past 'solutions' have further complicated political discussions and postponed any viable, and essential, debate on Mali's national equilibrium, especially at economic and political levels.

The extreme fragmentation of community interests, especially in the north, should encourage reflection on (i) the minimal model for inclusiveness (which groups and leaders are most representative among each community in order to enhance the presence of the state across the entire country) and (ii) the common denominator between all groups in terms of grievances and demands.

Economic and political rebellions, nationalistic postures and partial regional mediations have made discontent part of the structure of north-south relations, and eventually led to declining interest in the quite legitimate roots of the crisis. While rebel entrepreneurs (such as Iyad ag Ghali for instance) and some southern politicians share a common responsibility for the conflict, other actors have acted as 'passive co-producers' of tensions between north and south.

Regional interference and the regional leadership race between Algeria and Libya have played a part in aggravating the disagreements between Malian communities. Moreover, with increased security threats in the Sahel (trafficking, hostage taking, terrorist attacks), some Western countries have decided to tackle these issues directly and make Mali a stronghold of the international 'war(s) on terror'. This trend will be dealt with in the next chapter.

Chapter Three

Foreign powers involvement

While Mali has long been considered as a relative 'no interest' zone by the international community (because of its apparent democratic normality and the absence of strategic resources), other African countries, such as Libya and Algeria, have made this country, and the northern regions in particular, central to their Sahel leadership strategies. The inability of the Malian government to assert its political and military presence in the northern areas has greatly facilitated those foreign interferences. Amadou Toumani Touré's voluntary relinquishment of state sovereignty in some northern areas exacerbated that sense of impunity. At the same time, fragmentation between northern communities has provided Mali's neighbours with the ideal levers to establish their presence and/or their leadership in the region. For security, political or economic reasons, other countries in the region have used this area for their own gains, and thereby directly contributed to local instability and national tensions between north and south.

On the international side, the 9/11 terrorist attacks and the growing number of kidnappings of Westerners in the country since 2003 have progressively made the country a central point of implementation for new security doctrines. The United States and France, for instance, decided to significantly augment their security and military programmes in the region. Despite growing suspicion regarding collusion between the Malian regime, trafficking groups and bandits in the north, Bamako's authorities remain one of the main beneficiaries of foreign aid in the Sahel. However, by deliberately emphasising security issues and, as a consequence, setting aside other issues such as development or historical distrust between north and south, international programmes have fed the resentment between Malian communities.

This chapter addresses the roots of northern Mali's attraction to other regional powers and the consequences of foreign interests on local dynamics and national unity. It also details the security programmes that have been implemented in the region since the early 2000s and the lack of national ownership that have fostered tensions and precipitated the 2012 breakdown.

Regional interference based on geopolitical interest: Libya and Algeria

Since the 1960s, Tuareg rebellions and the gradual withdrawal of the Malian military from the north of Mali have fostered insecurity at national and regional levels. These armed struggles have created a 'political economy of violence' in northern border areas – and economy based on arms, human and drug trafficking, which has fed criminal and terrorist networks while corrupting political actors.

Regional neighbours have played a part in the implementation of this paradigm. While one would expect regional partners to try to diffuse the situation, evidence shows that some of them have taken advantage of insecurity in northern Mali to advance their own geopolitical interests.

Over the years, the north of Mali has became an area of strategic, economic and security interest for several regional powers, especially Libya and Algeria and, to a lesser extent, Morocco. While the influence of Morocco in northern Mali should not be downplayed, Libya and Algeria have been the most active players in the region over the past 30 years.

Libya increased its mediation and support for insurgencies in the region in order to extend its political (and ideological) control over Tuareg communities. Algeria mainly used northern Mali to export its internal security threats and to militarily secure its own territory. These two strategies have had deep effects on the already fragile equilibrium of northern post-colonial Mali.

Libya in Mali: support to rebels and patronage

The Libya of Colonel Qaddafi was involved in northern Mali as part of its greater ambition to control the Sahel. Animated by his desire to unify African countries around the Jamahiriya, Qaddafi set up the League of Grand Sahara Tribes project, which attracted the support of Tuareg communities eager to emancipate themselves from the control of the Malian state. In the same vein, Qaddafi actively participated in the creation of the CEN-SAD (Community of Sahel-Saharan States) in 1998. Initially comprising Libya, Sudan, Chad, Niger, Mali and Burkina Faso, it expanded to finally encompass 28 states in 2008 and even stretched beyond the Sahel-Saharan zone. CEN-SAD, however, always excluded Algeria. Over the years, Qaddafi used the enormous resources provided by Libyan oil to financially, militarily and politically support African rebellions, using them against his neighbours. Northern Mali was no exception to this strategy, as Muammar Qaddafi continuously alternated between supporting the Tuareg in their rebellious aspirations and mediating in the aftermath of uprisings.

The support Qaddafi gave to the Malian Tuareg (and the economic opportunities Libya provided to Malian economic refugees in the 1970s and

1980s) enabled him to recruit them into his Islamic Legion. This 'integration policy' was beneficial to both parties. On one hand, it allowed Qaddafi to build lasting allegiances with local populations in northern Mali while increasing his military power. The Tuaregs recruited into the Libyan army 'special units' were used by Qaddafi for his military projects (the war in Chad and Lebanon during the 1980s for instance). On the other hand, the recruited Tuareg soldiers hoped that the Libyan leader would financially and logistically back them once they were home again and making plans to rebel against the Malian government. However, this never materialised and the several Tuareg uprisings in Mali were launched with military equipment patiently gathered by the rebels rather than graciously provided by Qaddafi. The fall of his regime played a decisive role in the uprising in northern Mali.

For the Malian government, Libyan patronage presented an alternative to costly investments and somehow responded to consent-based sovereignty-sharing. The Libya of Muammar Qaddafi not only played a stabilising (and destabilising) political role with regard to the Tuareg rebellions, proposing mediation and sponsoring peace agreements (by, for instance, moving Tuareg rebel leaders out of northern Mali), it also greatly contributed to the Malian economy as assistance from Tripoli helped develop several economic sectors. Qaddafi paid for the construction of mosques, set up the Malian national television network in the 1980s, and financed the Malian government complex. Those investments gained him support from the Malian government and some sectors of the population.

Libyan investments in Mali were accompanied by a significant flow of economic migrants in the opposite direction. Since the droughts of the

1970s, the gradual collapse of the pastoral economy, and the political isolation of northern populations, generations of young people in search of employment have taken the route to Libya. There, these ishumars (derivative of the term chômeurs, or unemployed) engaged in trans-border activities, ranging from seasonal employment to informal or criminal trafficking. Those economic opportunities allowed northern Mali to survive difficulties 'through the financial and material flux allowed by the Libyan leader'. It was also in Libya that the ishumar protest culture was developed, infusing and unifying rebel Tuareg projects in the 1990s.

When Qaddafi's regime collapsed in 2011, Mali was deprived of one of its main political brokers and economic benefactors. Together with the heavy weapons that accompanied returning well-equipped and well-trained Tuareg 'vigilantes' of the Islamic Legion, this development precipitated the outbreak of the 2012 crisis.

But Libya was not the only country trying to impose its regional hegemony through northern Mali. Algeria, seeing the northern regions of Mali as its own backyard, regularly intervened in the internal affairs of its southern neighbour.

Algeria's natural backyard

Despite considering itself as the champion of anti-colonialism and anti-imperialism because of its constitutional doctrine of non-interference, Algeria never refrained from being involved in Malian affairs. The continuous rebellions in northern Mali actually offered Algiers the opportunity to establish itself as a responsible regional actor, as showcased by its many mediations between Bamako and the Tuareg rebels (Tamanrasset agreements in 1991, mediation in 1992, Algiers agreements in 2006 and also in 2015).

The diplomatic role Algiers wanted to play in order to assert its regional leadership also encouraged a strong mobilisation in the global fight against terrorism. Since its own civil war in the 1990s, Algeria has engaged in a ferocious counter-terrorist enterprise against domestic terrorist groups. This has not always been a success, as the Groupe Islamique Armé (GIA) and the Groupe Salafiste pour la Prédication et le Combat (GSPC) managed to make terrorist attacks against government targets on numerous occasions. This led the Algerian government to intensify its efforts and launch a repression and infiltration programme. That policy proved to be successful as it reduced the level of violence within Algeria and created tensions within the GSPC. The consequence of this success was a displacement of the terrorist threat to peripheral deserted areas, such as northern Mali. From there, the organisation began to operate in the Sahel region, making a living out of hostage-taking (mainly Western hostages) and trafficking.

The expansion of GSPC activities to sub-Saharan countries, with no comparable military capabilities (Mali, Niger, Mauritania), had deep destabilising effects. The allegiance of the GSPC to Al Qaeda in 2007 and its change of name to AQIM, increased the terrorist threat, as the organisation was now backed by a major terrorist network.

Moreover, Algeria's ambiguous posture in the region also had negative consequences on the stability of the Sahel. First, Algiers tried to set up a coordinated regional response to cross-border terrorism. This was highlighted by the signing of the Tamanrasset Plan in 2009 by Mali, Niger, Algeria and Mauritania, which led to the creation, in 2010, of a Comité d'Etat-Major Opérationnel Coinjoint in Tamanrasset (CEMOC – a joint military operations centre) and of a joint intelligence cell in Algiers (UFL). The effectiveness of CEMOC and the joint intelligence centre have been regularly questioned by some who argue that the arrangement was designed 'in part, to ward off Western military intervention in response to terrorist and criminal threats in the region'. Any external military intervention is seen by Algeria as a direct affront to its national sovereignty. Whether these assertions are accurate or not, Mali has directly suffered from the intensification of Algeria's domestic fight against terrorism.

Second, Algeria's counter-terrorism cooperation with regional countries, and especially with Mali, has remained limited and dependent on its own interests. Algiers, indeed, considered Bamako to be insufficiently committed to the fight against AQIM, too eager to facilitate the liberation of terrorist prisoners, and too quick to pay ransoms for Western hostages. Bamako, contrastingly, viewed Algiers as being unwilling to use its military superiority to capture AQIM cells that crossed Malian borders, despite the droit de poursuite conferred by Malian authorities. Some international observers even accused Algerian elements from the Departement du renseignement et de la sécurité (DRS) of 'leveraging control over military operations and influence within Tuareg communities to profit from lucrative Sahel smuggling operations'. Others argued that Algeria sought to dominate parts of the Sahel that could hold gas or mineral reserves.

The permanence of a terrorist threat in the Sahel and the de facto inability of countries in the region to address instability have encouraged other international partners, especially France and the US, to implement their own security strategies. However, rather than focusing on the root causes of insecurity and addressing economic tensions and political frustrations, the approach of the international community has indirectly contributed to a worsening of the situation. Mainly focused on fighting terrorist groups and traffickers, especially after the 9/11 terrorist attacks, international partners have neglected other aspects that could have prevented the insecurity from growing, for example supporting local economic development and involving Malian actors in order to create stability.

The security focus of the international community

The 9/11 terrorist attacks, the growing influence of the GSPC in northern Mali and the spread of a terrorist threat at the gates of Europe have contributed to decisive international engagement in the Sahel. The kidnappings of Westerners in 2003 highlighted the human costs and the potential economic consequences (supply of raw materials, especially uranium in Niger) of instability in the Sahel, and, therefore, encouraged unprecedented actions.

This section focuses on international programmes that have been implemented to fight terrorism and reduce insecurity in the Sahel. It evaluates their effects in the light of a negative Malian security assessment that culminated in the 2012 crisis.

The Sahel: from a terra nullius to a hotspot in the 'arc of crisis'

While the assessment of the global weakness of West African states (instability, porous borders, corruption) should have encouraged international partners to implement a comprehensive approach covering security and development issues, the US and France decided to pressure local countries mainly on matters of security. This military focus set aside a range of issues considered to be secondary, such as economic development, infrastructure investment or enhancement of the political representation of northern populations. International security incentives have, indeed, led to exclusively military-oriented programmes that, in some specific cases, bypassed national sovereignty. These included foreign intelligence and special forces acting in deserted areas of the Sahel.

Al Qaeda terrorist attacks in Western and African countries have made the Sahel a growing point of interest in terms of international security. West African states, especially Niger (which has been accused of selling uranium to Iraq) and Mali, decided to prevent criticisms and appear as resolute partners in the 'global war on terror'. One month after the 9/11 terrorist attacks, Malian authorities decided to expel 50 Pakistani preachers from Bamako. In northern Mali, worshipers from the Pakistani proselytising organisation Jama'at al Tabligh, especially Tuareg Ifoghas, were closely watched by Malian intelligence for their alleged connections with radical Islamic networks.

Between 2001 and the 2012 crisis, the international community initiated several security programmes and allocated hundreds of millions of dollars to the fight against terrorism, whether through intelligence, special forces, military training or equipment. Those unprecedented efforts proved unable to reverse the constant deterioration in regional security, especially since February 2003 when 32 Westerners were kidnapped (seized in Algeria and detained in Mali). That event confirmed the existence of a terrorist threat in the Sahel, and stimulated a global effort to address security issues in the region.

International plans to fight terrorism in northern Mali

In 2002, the United States Pan-Sahel Initiative was launched to address security and terrorist issues in the Sahel and help countries to ensure their own stability. Starting with $7 million and a limited focus on Mali, Mauritania, Niger and Chad, the US initiative progressively expanded and became, first in 2004, the Trans-Saharan Counter Terrorism Initiative (TSCTI, with a $500 million budget over six years) and then, in 2005, the Trans-Saharan Counter Terrorism Partnership (TSCTP, four-year budget of $288 million). The US programmes involved several components, including political (led by the Department of State), economic (USAID) and military actions ('Enduring Freedom' AFRICOM operation).

In 2008, France decided to launch its Plan Sahel in Mali, Niger and Mauritania, to fight terrorism and assist local development programmes. It allocated €58 million to the programme, which has now been extended to others countries in the Sahel with the goal of enhancing security coverage. The Plan Sahel was coupled with a quick reaction force (Operation Sabre) and a permanent military presence in Dakar (Sénégal) and Libreville (Gabon). The Plan Sahel inspired other initiatives, especially from the European Union with the launch in 2011 of the Strategy for Security and Development (€600 million for good governance, development and conflict prevention programmes).

The French and US initiatives have, however, turned out to be almost exclusively security oriented and, intentionally or not, served to sideline other issues that they had initially pledged to deal with.

Despite all these initiatives, Mali, for its part, only began to address security and development issues in 2010-2011. With financial support from the international community, the Special Programme for Peace, Security and Development in northern Mali (PSPSDN) was intended to assist the economic development of the north and prevent future destabilisation. Led by Mohamed ag Erlaf, a Tuareg Ifoghas from Kidal and a minister in the 1990s, the PSPSDN has been, quite ironically, a major cause of growing discontent in northern communities. With a €50 million budget, the PSPSDN was designed to address both security and development issues. The aim of the programme was to strengthen the capacities of the army (new garrisons and police stations) and, at the same time, create health centres, schools, grain banks, water supply, etc.

However, the programme turned out to be, once again, almost exclusively military-oriented and mainly managed through a southern diagnosis of the problems, featuring southern military units, excessive centralisation and the absence of local consultation. The PSPSDN has been extensively debated and contested, especially by a Tuareg advocacy network (Réseau plaidoyer en faveur de la paix, de la sécurité et du développement au Nord-Mali) led by Alghabass ag Intallah, deputy of Kidal and brother of the new Amenokal, the traditional chief of the Ifoghas community. Local communities were deeply disappointed by a programme they first considered to be an historic commitment, based on the 1992 Pacte national and 2006 Algiers peace agreement, to northern populations. The creation of 'Poles sécurisés de développement et de gouvernance' without local consultation and the disproportionate resources allocated to security programmes instead of to development deeply sullied the image of the PSPSDN. In the end, the programme was seen by northern communities as a new attempt from Bamako to dominate the northern regions and impose an exogenous political order, therefore exacerbating northern resentment.

Security without trust: the failure of the fight against terrorism in northern Mali

The 2012 crisis also emphasised the discrepancy between international security efforts and the capabilities of the Malian security apparatus. The success of international assistance in addressing the security situation or supporting local ownership of military matters has been questioned. The speed and ease with which the armed groups took the northern cities between January and March 2012 has demonstrated both the weakness of the security programmes that have been implemented so far and the shortcomings of available (and shared) intelligence data regarding the resources and activity of terrorist organisations.

By marginalising contacts and good relations with local communities, the central government and its international partners have, in the end, weakened local ownership of the security programmes, which also explains the support given to armed groups by local populations. Islamist groups, indeed, have acted as a social security provider, fulfilling roles that the Malian government has been unable to deliver to northern population –

for example, medical and food aid, schooling, financial donations for marriages, and fuel.

Ransoms, political deals (exchanging hostages for prisoners) and electoral bargains (withdrawal of the Malian army from the north before the 2007 presidential elections) have also played major roles in undermining the security situation. In each case, they have fed local hostility towards national and international authorities and delayed the search for alternatives until it was too late.

Conclusion

Regional political and security interference in the Sahel played a major part in the lead-up to the 2012 crisis. By feeding rebellions through political support, economic assistance and military supply, or by fostering internal divisions within the northern communities, foreign countries bear significant responsibility for insecurity in the Sahel. As a wide-open political and social ecosystem, northern Mali has been highly vulnerable to foreign interference. The weakness of the Malian state and the biased lenses through which southern authorities saw northern issues, encouraged interference by other countries. Moreover, Algiers and Tripoli considered Mali as a strategic area for their leadership disputes.

The evolution of the international security paradigm generated by the 9/11 terrorist attacks has led to the involvement of new international actors in the Sahel region. The huge growth in criminal and terrorist activities, coupled with constant threats against Western nationals, culminated in the launch of heavily subsided programmes. However, the exclusive focus on security undermined the efficiency of those strategies, and had some unintended consequences for West African countries.

Some of these programmes, indeed, been used by local (i.e., southern) elites to consolidate their leadership positions. Overall, the Malian strategic 'use' of security rents for domestic purposes and the political domination of the northern desert areas have aggravated the long-standing tensions between the central government and northern communities.

Conclusions

Finding solution to the recurrent crisis?

Just as the last three Malian crises failed to result in any viable settlement, but instead progressively deepened levels of distrust between the country's various communities, the 2012 conflict is seriously testing the resolve and the creativity of local and international bodies. As is plainly evident from recent history, military solutions and a counter-terrorism commitment in the Sahel are not sufficient in themselves to generate long-term stability in the region. Alongside these security initiatives, political dialogue and economic development need to remain a central part of the Malian normalisation process.

In addition to general efforts that must be made in terms of basic infrastructure (for instance, in social services and transport), youth unemployment, and political representation to foster national 'reconciliation', tensions between communities must also be addressed. Since independence in 1960, Mali's precarious national unity has been built upon conflict and distrust between communities. Even within Tuareg and Arab clans, schisms and rifts have significantly weakened the political impact of rebellions and encouraged a policy of divide-and-rule by the central state.

However, contrary to past crises, the 2012 conflict also introduced deep divisions between secular and separatist movements (such as the MNLA) and radical Islamic groups with strong links to international terrorist coalitions and foreign sponsors (the case of Ansar Dine). This has complicated analysis of the conflict and the search for quick and viable responses.

Featuring two different 'platforms' of non-state armed groups and six different 'representative' groups (excluding several other terrorist organisations and community militias that are not present), the ongoing Algiers peace talks perfectly illustrate this complexity. Difficulties in addressing all the demands and identifying a common denominator between all participants have led to several delays in the negotiations.

Divisions within the mediation team, largely resulting from Algeria's dominant role, and, before that, the growth in the number of regional and international initiatives, have also pushed back the start of the negotiation process. This lost time has played a significant role in furthering divisions between armed groups. It has also contributed to radicalising positions on both sides of the table, and giving the 'most sovereign', separatist and radicalised factions greater sway at the expense of more moderate positions.

All 'representative' actors and donors generally agree on the economic, political and security reforms needed to solve the crisis and address Malian issues over the long term. However, because they are too complex or too local, questions of local (i.e., Malian) ownership and incentives have been regularly sidelined in the stabilisation processes.

How might foreign partners support the Malian stabilisation process by pooling their efforts more effectively? How could Malian history help north and south reach a new form of settlement that is acceptable to all sides and bring about long-term stability in the country?

International coordination as a first step to normalisation

The Tuareg rebellion in January 2012 and the military coup in March have brought into question not only Malian stability as a whole but also the capacity of international partners and/or regional leaders to manage a major crisis and to address, at one and the same time, a security conflict and a political breakdown.

ECOWAS, the African Union, the United Nations, the European Union and all of Mali's bilateral partners have not fully succeeded in aligning their views and agreeing on a consensual solution. No fewer than six different mediators, High/Special representatives or Special Envoys have been involved in the Malian crisis, sometimes with no specific knowledge of Malian dynamics or local networks. Some of them have also been 'bypassed' by concurrent initiatives, either from their own organisation or by other private actors. None of those divided efforts succeeded either in quickly setting the main priorities or in exerting the necessary pressure on the junta or the northern armed groups, especially the MNLA and Ansar Dine – approaches that might have prevented undesired developments such as the radical Islamist occupation of the northern cities, and divisions between the main groups in the rebellion. The Ouagadougou agreement between the Malian interim government and representatives of the armed groups was only signed in June 2013, a year after the Islamist occupation of the north and several months after the launch of French-African military operations (Serval, MISMA, on 11 January 2013).

During that time, Mali's interim authorities were weakened: President Traoré fled the country for medical treatment in May 2012 after being lynched by pro-junta members. On the northern front, the MNLA became marginalised by other groups, especially Ansar Dine and its allies from AQIM and MUJAO, which had more resources and were able to poach some low-paid combatants. Disunity inside the international community indirectly helped to change the nature of the Malian conflict.

Moreover, the inappropriate selection of mediators has had profound consequences on local politics. The choice of President Blaise Compaoré as a mediator, for instance, was interpreted as provocative, given the difficult historical relationship between Burkina and Mali (the two wars of 1974 and 1985), and Ouagadougou's hidden political agenda in the region (support of political opposition, and destabilising interference).

While the presidential elections in July and August 2013 were supposed to prevent further destabilisation on the political side and give a new impulse to conflict resolution, they instead encouraged nationalistic postures and the questioning of foreign engagement. President

Keita insisted on several occasions on the necessity of a Malian peace process, denouncing external interference and Burkina Faso's alleged support for rebel armed groups. By openly advocating a greater role for Morocco – for which IBK's election had constituted a great opportunity after decades of tensions, and the most practical way to counterbalance Algeria's regional leadership – Bamako disavowed international efforts. By eventually accepting the Algerian mediation proposal a few months later (15 January 2014), the president not only discarded the Moroccan strategy for dealing with the MNLA (a secular separatist group), but also denied the role that international appointed representatives (from the ECOWAS, the AU or the UN) were meant to play in the political process.

The Ouagadougou agreement, the Moroccan meetings, the MINUSMA's workshops, other bilateral initiatives and private efforts to facilitate crisis resolution paradoxically served to delay political rapprochement between north and south. The Algiers peace process (which started in April 2014) put an end to these poorly coordinated initiatives, but at the same time marginalised the existing mediation mandates. Moreover, with its fourth mediation in a Malian conflict since 1991, Algiers succeeded in imposing its leadership and 'eliminating' competition from other regional candidates. Even so, Algeria's diplomatic comeback is still questioned in light of its general neutrality in the 2012 conflict and its past failure to support a long-term peace in Mali.

Besides the recent efforts undertaken to secure a viable peace agreement, the effectiveness of international long-term strategies in the region could also be questioned, especially regarding the large number of current initiatives and the lack of coordination between them. The French military operation Barkhane, the current updating of international strategies for development and security (French Plan Sahel, US Trans-Saharan Counter-Terrorism Programme, the EU strategy) and new multilateral programmes (such as UN or World Bank global strategies) might well point to the future divisions of labour between international actors in the Sahel. Insufficient synergy and increasing numbers of interlocutors could undermine clear support for stabilisation in Mali, and encourage local divisions over the main priorities to address – whether security, economic development or political reform.

Mistakes, uncoordinated efforts, contradictory messages and blurry priorities have complicated the prospects for dialogue and delayed a general consensus on the viable stabilisation of Mali. The time might have come to encourage endogenous and comprehensive approaches that could sustain long-term peace in Mali and the stabilisation process in the Sahel region.

Endogenous solutions to the Malian crisis

As a diverse society, Mali has always been confronted with cultural heterogeneity and local conflicts. Even though recent history highlights the tensions that exist within the Malian national community, other examples based on ancient traditions of conflict prevention could, in contrast, serve as way out of the crisis and support dialogue between conflicting communities. In order to maintain political unity, local authorities have historically developed tools of conflict prevention. Mali's political culture could, as a consequence, be a great addition to international efforts and could help implement local and global stabilisation strategies.

From the constitution of the Malian Empire in 1235 to the post-colonial Tuareg rebellions, the Malian central state has always had to deal with plurality and community tensions. However, in order to put an end to community conflicts and give the Malian state a 'national' unity, local authorities have used several methods to neutralise tensions and give to the numerous communities a common ground of understanding of peaceful cohabitation. The 'joke relationships' formula (Sinankuya or cousinage à plaisanterie) institutionalised by Soundjata Keita in the 13th century in order to dampen tensions between communities is one of the most symbolic, and still effective, methods.

Cousinage is part of popular culture across the whole of West Africa. Even if the Sinankuya system has been partly perverted by the 'democratisation' process (which downplayed the importance of traditional groups and encouraged political use of this banter for electoral purposes), it could still be a useful tool for conflict prevention and inter-community dialogue.

Among other local 'innovations' that could fulfil a stabilising role in forthcoming years, the 'grins' might be an effective way to foster dialogue and bring the central state and northern communities closer together. Created in the 18th century near Ségou (100km away from Bamako), the grins gather people, most of the time men, from the same age cohort to discuss or share social activities.

Grins are still one of the most efficient means for political, religious or social leaders to 'take the temperature' and communicate their intentions. Every political leader is connected to a specific grin, which he can lead (chef de grin), or not. During Amadou Toumani Touré's regime (2002-2012), his grin was one of the most popular and prestigious in Bamako: any Malian who wanted to see or talk to the president outside the Koulouba palace tried to attend the grin. During the 2007 general elections, Ibrahim Boubacar Keita was heavily criticised for recurrent absence at his grin. Even today, #grin223 is one of the most popular requests on Twitter for people who want to be informed of the latest news.

Even though the 'contemporary' grins can sometimes only be seen as places where young unemployed people kill time by playing cards and drinking tea, or where politicians go to give out bribes, their political influence is still very important, especially in urban areas. They can be the starting point of popular discontent. But, by giving the young, elders and unemployed people a free space to discuss and even criticise the prevailing political, economic or religious powers, they also have a positive effect on the regulation of social tensions. As a consequence, grins are normative and operational reference points for discussion and dialogue, and could be part of the global stabilisation process, especially in terms of a bottom-up approach to the crisis.

Last, but not least, the long tradition of political dialogue and religious tolerance in Mali could encourage endogenous strategies designed to foster community inclusiveness and stabilisation. The collegial formula of power and the principle of political coalition have fed Malian political history for a long time (with varying uccess, despite the poor reputation it gained under the ATT presidency of). Through their association with dignitaries (federated clans, militaries or comrades-in-arms in the case of the Malian Empire, Talibes for the Toucouleur confederation, traders during Samory Touré's reign, or Marabouts at the time of the Macina Empire), Malian leaders have strengthened the state and reinforced national unity. But religion has also played a very important role in this nation-building process. When 95 percent of the 15 million inhabitants in Mali are Muslims, religious leaders represent an indisputable element of political order and social mobilisation. The 2009 debate on the proposal for a new family code clearly illustrated the strength of religious values in Malian society. It confirmed the need to meet with religious and traditional representatives to consult on changes in state policy and social reforms, and to use them as advocates in support of stability.

The large audiences attracted by religious representatives such as Mohamed Ould Cheickna Hamaoula (Chérif de Nioro), Cheikh Cherif Ousmane Madani Haidara (head of the Malekite movement), Imam Mahmoud Dicko (head of the High Islamic Council) and other popular preachers (Bandiougou Doubia, Soufi Bilali, etc) could encourage a broader dialogue on the main objectives of the stabilisation process and/or the favoured ways out of the 2012 crisis. Considering the absence of true Islamic radicalisation in the country and, in that context, the need to implement more culturally grounded solutions to the crisis, religious and traditional actors could usefully assist Malian authorities.

If political authorities gave religious leaders a symbolic role in future national dialogue, alongside other relevant 'moral figures', the Malian government could maximise opportunities for long-term stability or, at the least, prevent any strong opposition in society.

Re-legitimating the Malian state

While decentralisation is seen as a panacea and the only viable solution to Mali's long-term stabilisation, acceptance by local communities remains essential to any effort to strengthen and extend the Malian state. Imposing the central state on peripheral regions, sometimes with military means, has been one of the major causes of northern discontent for decades. While some northern representatives have been co-opted by Bamako in order to enhance Mali's local legitimacy, they have mostly been heavily criticised and locally disowned. Mohamed ag Erlaf's appointment as national coordinator of the PSPSDN was a clear illustration of that response. Under these circumstances, how could state presence in desert areas be re-invented, and what would be the best way to represent northern interests in Bamako's institutions?

Decentralisation instantly appears as one of the most viable solutions. However, since the first post-colonial regime of Modibo Keita, decentralisation programmes have been embezzled by southern and/or some northern elites and never directly benefitted local populations through better infrastructure or public services. Decentralisation remains one of the few options seemingly available to anchor the Malian state in the north and legitimate national identity in the peripheral regions. Other means, however, could provide opportunities to address the general issue of Bamako's lack of legitimacy and provide effective responses to peripheral frustration and political misunderstandings.

One first line of approach would be to reform some of the existing institutions in order to make them more representative of Malian diversity, or more effective in improving the living conditions of local populations. Since 1992, for instance, the Haut Conseil des Collectivités Territoriales (HCCT) is meant to represent regional interests and Malian communities in the political decision-making process. However, because of its 'consultative' status and the indirect election of its members, the HCCT has never succeeded in shifting Bamako's policy framework towards the north or legitimising the central state among northern groups, especially the Tuareg and Arabs. An electoral reform of the Council and more constitutional responsibilities for its members could improve HCCT efficiency and include regional interests more significantly in national policy. If a proposed 'second chamber' in Mali could be mainly regarded an opportunity for local leaders to access new economic rents, it could also be a way for local populations to be better represented and better informed on national policy (and programmes), and/or, more prosaically, to increase their access to some form of state-based income.

Another, and less cumbersome, option could be to give to Malian traditional leaders a legal role and, as already exists in Niger and Burkina Faso, some consultative prerogative on specific and possibly contentious issues. Traditional leaders generally have a moral role that could give them natural authority, and could be used to regulate tensions between communities. In Mali, because of the involvement of some traditional leaders with the dictatorial regime, democratic authorities have never allowed them to play an official role in the political field. Alongside political representatives and other moral authorities (religious leaders mainly), traditional chiefs could nevertheless play a positive role in managing tensions and streamlining relationships between local populations and the central state.

Regional examples could usefully inspire Malian authorities in that sense and help them to implement the current stabilisation process. Sharing a common history and ethnic similarities with Mali, Niger has also experienced several episodes of regional violence but, contrary to Mali, has succeeded in managing these tensions with creative solutions and innovative forms of inclusivity. In 2004, in order to end rebellions and prevent political issues from further destabilising the country, authorities decided, with the help of the United Nations (Agadez forum), to create a national council for political dialogue (CNDP). Jointly led by the majority and the opposition leaders, and placed under the patronage of Grands témoins (religious leaders, traditional chiefs), the council gathers all the existing political parties and relevant organisations to address a specific issue. It may be convened at the request of one of its members and only makes consensual recommendations. However, those recommendations are always proposed to government and then to the National Assembly, which can decide whether or not to legislate. Since its creation, the CNDP has successfully resolved many issues that could have otherwise led to a crisis or an exacerbation of tensions among parties (e.g., on electoral census, political zoning, electoral law, etc). The CNDP has greatly contributed to Niger's stability and to central state legitimacy across the territory. It has so far facilitated the dialogue between Niamey and peripheral regions, and allowed those regions to draw the attention of the government to specific issues.

Because of similarities between the two countries, the model of the CNDP could be easily reproduced in the Malian context. Moreover, Mali already has similar, though fewer, institutional experiences throughout its recent political history. The Democratic Appeal Spaces (Espaces d'interpellation démocratique), for instance, which were established in 1992, first succeeded in strengthening communication between the government and Malian citizens or civil associations after the first democratic elections. It helped the democratic authorities to familiarise populations with the new constitutional rules. Later, the model of Regional Concertation Spaces (Espaces de concertation régionale) and the Bamako Table Ronde, led in 1998 by Prime Minister Ibrahim Boubacar Keita, also gave the government the opportunity to secure the regime after the litigious elections of 1997 and to prevent any further destabilisation from the radical opposition that boycotted the scrutiny (Coalition of Opposition Political Parties – COPPO). By gathering representatives of the state, political parties, religious bodies, members of civil society and the diplomatic corps (370 participants), those exercises aimed to discuss the constitutional texts and to revise some litigious rules (creation of a parliamentary opposition status, authorisation of independent candidacies, etc) in order to foster political acceptance of the regime.

Those ad hoc or permanent tools could now help make the national authorities accountable to the local populations and develop lines of communications with all interested parties on a given issue. By establishing a new arena of supra-political dialogue, and giving a new responsibility in global stability to historically ignored groups, Malian authorities could foster the stabilisation process and help their own national legitimisation.

Mali's path to stability calls for innovative solutions and creative ways to re-invent the presence of the state across the territory. Ancient or contemporary endogenous models, examples from neighbouring countries or reform of some existing institutions could lead to peace in the long run and to trust between communities.

CPSIA information can be obtained
at www.ICGtesting.com
Printed in the USA
LVHW040547020920
664727LV00019B/957